NEW JERSEY
UFOs

New Jersey

UFOs

GERARD J. MEDVEC

4880 Lower Valley Road • Atglen, PA 19310

Designed by Danielle D. Farmer
Type set in Compacta Bd BT / Gill Sans

ISBN: 978-0-7643-4622-4
Printed in The United States

Schiffer Books are available at special discounts for bulk purchases for sales promotions or premiums. Special editions, including personalized covers, corporate imprints, and excerpts can be created in large quantities for special needs. For more information contact the publisher:

Published by Schiffer Publishing, Ltd.
4880 Lower Valley Road
Atglen, PA 19310
Phone: (610) 593-1777; Fax: (610) 593-2002
E-mail: Info@schifferbooks.com

For the largest selection of fine reference books on this and related subjects, please visit our website at
www.schifferbooks.com.
We are always looking for people to write books on new and related subjects. If you have an idea for a book, please contact us at proposals@schifferbooks.com.

This book may be purchased from the publisher.
Please try your bookstore first.
You may write for a free catalog.

Front cover image:
Alien attack. UFO over forest the sunset sky © galdzer. Courtesy of www.bigstockphoto.com.

DEDICATION

This book is for my beautiful wife, Joyce,
my soul mate and frontline editor of every written word.
And to all those who told their tales from one of my
favorite places on earth, and former home—New Jersey.

ACKNOWLEDGMENTS

Thanks to Karen, the research associate at the International UFO Museum and Research Center in Roswell, New Mexico, for her kind and quick help with information on sightings in New Jersey. To Peter Davenport for allowing rewrites from the National UFO Report Center files. To George Filer for permission to rewrite several reports from Filer's Files. To my editor and hypnotist, Dinah Roseberry, for patience and guidance. To the MUFON chapter in Philadelphia and the New York City UFO Meet-Up Group, for allowing me to join their fine organizations despite the distances. Thanks to Pat Marcattileo, and all the great people in The New Jersey and Pennsylvania UFO S.E.T.I. Group, Hamilton, New Jersey. Also to Sally Miller and The UFO Group of Hunterdon County, New Jersey, for delightful and intelligent talk.

EPIGRAPH

"We have found a strange footprint
on the shores of the unknown."

—Arthur Eddington
British astrophysicist

CONTENTS

NORTH JERSEY
-Sussex, -Passaic, -Bergen
-Warren, -Morris, -Essex
-Hudson, Union, Hunterdon
-Somerset, Middlesex
-Mercer, Monmouth

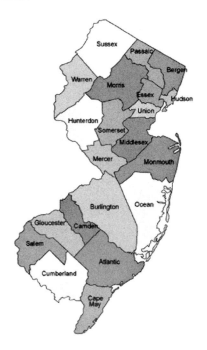

SOUTH JERSEY
-Burlington, Ocean, Camden
-Atlantic, Gloucester, Salem
-Cumberland, , Cape May

Map of North and South Jersey

INTRODUCTION

Thanks for opening this book.

"New Jersey and *UFOs*: Perfect Together" could be an updated version of former Governor Tom Kean's advertisements from 2009 relaying "New Jersey and You: Perfect Together."

It would certainly fit.

Collecting stories about extraterrestrial/inter-dimensional goings-on from citizens of the Garden State was not that difficult. Many people have seen many things in New Jersey, and for whatever reasons, they are being compelled to get their tales out to the public. This would be not only eye-opening for the reader, but also cathartic for the story-sharer.

New Jersey UFOs, like my previous two UFO books (*Mid-Atlantic UFOs: High Traffic Area,* and *UFOs Above PA,* with co-author Mark Sarro) is not about convincing anyone that UFOs are real. For any firsthand experiencer like me, it is no longer a question whether aliens are here or not. *They are here.* And no one can take that knowledge away. These stories reinforce that knowledge, and help those who are unsure to see the bigger picture through eyewitness scenarios, whether it be a simple globe flying around in a field, an abduction, or something in between. *New Jersey UFOs* has all of that.

But there is more.

The stories are also about *heart,* the human heart and its bewilderment, reaction, and long-term adjustment after some form of alien happening. An attempt has been made to give the reader a shared feeling with the witnesses, to take part in the event via the printed page and to come away with an expanded outlook on the world. This is not a nuts-and-bolts-only read-through (though there are twenty-five *short reports* that will give you that type of information). As happens in real life, mixed with the facts are the emotional and mental scrambling of the earthling. A UFO need only show-up once and the observer has learned something magnanimous with which they must struggle; they now live in an ultra-complex universe partly occupied by beings of superior intelligence.

The UFO reality is the biggest deal to ever grace this planet. But small things are still important.

Some technical notes: The great state of New Jersey, for this book, is divided into two sections: north and south. The accompanying map shows which counties are assigned to each section. I know there is usually a Central New Jersey in most references to the Garden State, so I hope the nice folk in those counties will forgive my rearrangement for simplicity's sake.

For the hard-core UFO watchers who love to travel to places written about in books to try to duplicate the experiences, here is an important note. The following stories have been moved from their real-life locations to different ones for privacy's sake: "Character Sketch," "God's Country," "Does Rain Matter," "East and West," "Green Backs," and "Head-on." Does it matter that the locations have changed? Not one bit. Because of the huge number of sightings being reported, I believe UFOs are visible somewhere over *every neighborhood in every part of the world, almost every night.* (See my previous book *Mid-Atlantic UFOs: High Traffic Area.* The introduction enumerates over five sightings per day in the Mid-Atlantic region alone. And these are only the *reported sightings* from only two official websites. They do *not* include the much larger number of UFO observations that are never reported—like *my own thirty-five occurrences.*) In my opinion then, you have as good a chance of seeing a UFO in the areas written about in the above six stories as you would in any of the other stories, or as you would anywhere else on Earth.

All full-length stories are in a short-story format, just as in my previous books. This means I have taken small liberties with some *minuscule* details in order to make the stories more fun to read. However, *the UFO facts, be they mine or other UFO witnesses, are untainted and remain in the experiencer's own words.*

I believe in every one of the stories that follow, if only because my *personal experiences corroborate the potential for all of them to be true.* More than that, each story was told voluntarily, with conviction, with passion, from people who had nothing to gain except their tale being published (all *anonymously* except for one person) and hopefully read by folk who care.

Many of the interviewees for this book told multiple stories. Often the stories bounce around to different parts of New Jersey and cross the fictitious north-south line mentioned earlier. As important as the sightings themselves, I feel, are the people who have seen them. Therefore, I have elected to keep an individual's stories together under their initial tale. That way one can garner an opinion of their extent of involvement with alien issues, and I hope one can also gain a broader image of the person.

In my previous two books, I've included a number of my own stories. I have one in here, also. But there could have been two. Actually, I spent two days camping at Belleplain State Park on the southern edge of the Pine Barrons in South Jersey for the specific reason of doing some UFO watching. And while I did not see anything in the park proper, I *did* find two UFOs on a side trip to a Wawa convenience store in Dennisville, New Jersey. Each of the alien globes were floating above the water, on separate nights, at the southeast corner of Johnson Pond near the bridge on Route 47 South, as you entered the town of Dennisville. The first one was a luminous, light blue orb. When I went back a week later to verify if it was still there (making it a human-made light), it was *not* there, *making it a UFO!* And—*something else* was there that second night: a bright orange globe at a slightly different location over the water, *that had not been there the previous time*, making *that* orange globe a UFO! Two UFOs in the same location on two different nights!

To anyone who has not experienced ET stuff yet in their life, this brief note may sound like a truly worthwhile story that should be fleshed-out within the confines of this book.

Frankly, there is only one reason for me *not* to include the story: *all* the stories that you are about to read are much, much better!

—Gerard J. Medvec

SOUTH JERSEY

Chapter 1

THE MAN FROM MARS
Washington Township, Bergen County

"Your fortune is not something to find but to unfold."

—Eric Butterworth
Senior Minister of The Unity Center of New York City

Bob froze.

The ominous black triangular craft he saw crept across the night sky, unidentifiable.

It was July 17, 1999, 9 p.m. on S. Mars Drive in Washington Township. A moment earlier, eighteen year-old Bob, following parental orders, had dragged a deadweight old bookcase from the den to their suburban curb in the hopes some local would haul it away for free. A lighter, sleeker bookcase was already installed to hold the increasing number of military DVDs, CDs, and books that were preparatory aids to Bob's dream of entering the Air Force Academy.

Bob dreamed every night about many things. While he had the uncanny ability to remember his dreams for months, or even years, he was not a "dreamer." Bob was a fact-based kind of guy. *Facts* were his friends, and the charcoal triangle he spotted overhead needed to provide some, because the aircraft designs and their lighting patterns that he had studied in books did not fit the visual before him.

But Bob also cherished the speculative. He loved the idea that other beings, everything from ghosts to extraterrestrials, inhabited our existence. Nocturnal imaginings often whisked him away to alien planets and saucer-filled invasions.

Despite the long-term memory of most of his dreams, Bob was not one to follow their whimsical suggestions. He would become a balancer of the physical and the unseen.

It began that Saturday night with a black triangle in the sky, drifting between fact and *para*-fact.

Bob shoved the furniture to the curb, turned back towards the house, and stopped dead.

There was a collection of three lights in the sky. One bright white light was in each corner of the triangle along with a dim red light in the center of its underbody. The color of the ship was dark gray against the dark sky, and its size was about that of a tennis ball held at arm's length. The edges of the craft were flat and had depth, perhaps ten feet or more. From the earth, it sat about 750 to 1,000 feet up, but that was only a guess. The machine did not match any of the configurations published in any of Bob's books or DVDs about current Air Force planes or copters.

At first sight, Bob did not take the triangle seriously. Perhaps it was a giant kite being flown at night with three…no, that could *not* be it. Nobody puts a light on their kite: that would make it too heavy. Besides, it was not windy enough to lift a kite. Maybe it was a reflection of some kind. A reflection would not stop, however, at about 1,000 feet and form a solid, sharp-edged appearance. It would travel infinitely upward or until it hit a cloud. And what on Earth would give a sharp, black triangular reflection with a light in each corner and one in the center?

His heart-felt feeling was: *this is weird.*

Then his pre-Air Force training hit gear and shoved his mind into mental note-taking and evaluation. The surroundings in the air and on the ground were studied. It was a partly cloudy night, with the moisture puffs high, wispy, and transparent. There was no jet engine noise, no propeller sounds, and the craft moved too slowly to be a conventional plane, because it would have fallen out of the sky. Nor was this a helicopter. There was no spinning tail rotor. No main rotors were visible. If the machine had had rotors, they would have been as long as a football-field, stirred the wind like a tornado, and bellowed louder than an atomic blast. The triangle was silent.

Oddly, this UFO was leading with one of the long, flat edges of the triangle, not with a point, as any human aircraft would do. Using aerodynamics, a human craft would want the point to lead to cut the air. The triangle craft, in essence, flew backwards. Human crafts cannot do that.

Once the details began to pile up, the reality of the sighting flushed his system clean. UFO.

That is when he noticed the hum.

A low tone, like a throbbing wave coursed through his body. Even the air seemed to shake with uncertainty. The feeling from the hum was less about sound and more about vibration. It continued until the craft coasted out of sight.

During this event nature had gone mute. There were no dogs barking, no insect sounds, no wind, nothing. Once the object left, which only took a few minutes, all these natural noises returned.

He dashed indoors and told his parents about the UFO. They were supportive.

Bob had experienced something new, something that few humans had ever seen. And he liked it.

That summer night saw the opening volley of a lifelong badminton game: Bob vs. Universe.

By age twenty-three, Bob had dropped desires for military marches so he could hug the life of a paranormal devotee. His war-like library had evolved from info on stringent bed-making techniques and Stealth Bomber capabilities, to include university studies of out-of-body experiences and collections of UFO histories and firsthand reports.

His love of the three dimensions, though, had not diminished. His college training was in something no less concrete than information technology. He could program and run computers blindfolded. Still, he would temper his physical life with ideas ethereal, and try hard to ground in logic the paranormal tales he came across.

But Bob's judicious scale was about to be superheated and twisted into a pile of conflicting concepts.

On the evening of February 24, 2002, Bob was coming home from his girlfriend's house, excited about their fun relationship. He was sure someday they would marry.

His black Ford Bronco rolled along the Black Horse Pike in Washington Township towards a restful night in the garage. He had stopped at a red left-turn signal. The rock group Queen was blasting on the tape player and the next song was about to begin. A large blue pickup truck lumbered behind him, sporting extended side mirrors.

The light changed green. Bob's car made the left turn – and something went extremely wrong. Life lost all logic. The blue pickup, behind him a second earlier, was now several hundred feet ahead of him! And the song that had just begun on the tape player was over and another song was starting.

How could this happen? Bob's nerves danced under his skin. His car was still making the left turn and moving down the street and he *was* driving it, but he felt like he had been yanked out of a trance and left with a muzzy hangover.

How did that truck get ahead of him? It was impossible.

Panic filled him, fed by terror. Tremors rippled his anatomy like a pond pommeled with footsteps. A temptation was to jump from the car and run. But he did not know where to, or why he felt he needed to do something so preposterous.

Then his military-like observation powers flamed on. He did not crash. The truck was still nearby, so why not *catch* him and ask *him* what happened. There was about three-and-a-half minutes missing. But the truck was only ten seconds in front of him. What the hell?

Bob's conclusion: somehow, more time passed *inside* his car than passed for the *rest of the world*.

Bob pursued the truck for a couple of miles, trying to get the driver to pull over with a few honks and arm waving out the window. He wanted to talk with the driver, but not seem like a paranoid stalker. The truck driver's perspective of what happened would be invaluable.

But the truck would not stop.

After turning into a large housing development, the truck scurried through a labyrinth of small streets and parking lots and was gone, no doubt concerned about the "nut" that was following him.

Feeling disappointed and a little nutty, Bob headed home, perplexed, but eager to write out the event on paper and begin an evaluation. Since he knew all the songs on the Queen tape by memory, he worked out easily that three-and-a-half minutes exactly were lost. Amazingly, he was at the wheel of a moving vehicle the whole time in an (apparently) unconscious state, yet he perfectly executed the left turn, had his foot on the gas, and did *not* have an accident. How does one do that?

Bob linked this frightening event to abduction missing time anomalies only because he could find nowhere else to connect a dot. Though he was reasonably sure that he was *not* abducted that night, other experiencers and scientists theorize in their books and papers that the aliens can do pretty much whatever they want, including, in theory, taking a passenger right off a bus, putting him through a battery of tests, and returning him a millisecond later without anyone on the bus, including the abductee, being the wiser.

Did that happen to Bob?

Do alien visitors so effortlessly manipulate time and space? The only one who could answer that would be the alien instigators themselves, and perhaps a handful of high-ranking officials in several earth-bound governments. The aliens would have to be asked that question face-to-face, a difficult, maybe dangerous endeavor. Then, too, would they tell you the truth? Either way, everyone else's opinion is a guess.

Bob's evaluation of his confounded-time problem found no answers, but he would never give up looking.

Shortly after this incident, between March and May of 2002, he began to change. Superman he did *not* become, but it seemed that his lost-time incident somehow boosted his psychic abilities. His sixth sense became augmented and little sparkles of insight began to manifest. He knew who was calling on the phone before he answered. The next song to play on the radio he could easily predict. His dreams became accurate premonitions of events that took place in reality soon after the dream occurred.

While these capabilities played a harmless, sometimes amusing song in his life, other changes were a dark cacophony. Many mornings he awoke from a quiet night's rest only to find spots of blood on the bed or his clothes and, sporadically, his skin. However, no punctures or cuts were ever located anywhere on his body, and there were zero indications that any blood had dripped from his mouth, nose, eyes, or ears.

But the morning of Wednesday, May 15, 2002, found a physical anomaly more peculiar than anything else he had experienced so far. He awoke that morning to find on the inside of his lower left leg, a *neat, triangular-shaped bruise* (see photos).

The natural first question was "what did I bang into?" Nothing triangular in the bruise's dimensions could be found anywhere that low to the ground at home, work, or other places he frequented. The mark did not hurt and was not sensitive to touch like every other bruise he had every received.

And then, seven days later, the bruise vanished. Unlike most bruises that change color gradually over the healing period, from a black-blue to a light yellow, the triangle bruise went from black-blue to completely gone overnight.

And in their place were four punctured wounds in a straight line: small, red, and raised. Bob had no explanation.

Though he was concerned about these bizarre marks, a doctor was not visited at the time since there was no pain with the condition, and Bob clung to the belief that these marks were natural results of bumps or insect bites. So he resorted to over-the-counter ingredients for a cure.

They were ineffective.

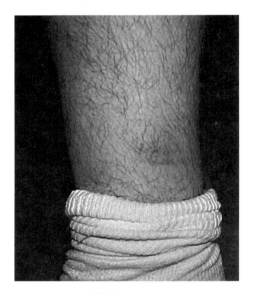

Initial leg mark.

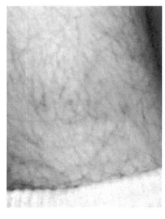

Close-up of same image.
Note triangular outline.

Another view.

During the ensuing week after the punctures had appeared, they were getting no better, so Bob finally elicited the help of a podiatrist friend in Paterson, New Jersey, who was also a ufologist. The following week, Bob was in his office. He relayed only the bare facts to the doctor, carefully omitting any feelings or speculation of his own.

An ultrasound test was completed (see photos) along with a dozen other procedures, including x-rays, in order to identify the odd marks. Tests results were surprising.

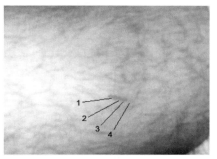

Puncture wounds that appeared a week later.

The doctor's analysis was that something had penetrated the skin, cut a piece of the tendon and removed it, and then inserted an "object" in the removed piece's place beneath the four punctures, connecting the tendons to both ends of "it." There was no inflammation, no irritation, and no scar tissue. His body had not reacted to this surgery, as if making a conscious decision to ignore it. The podiatrist was overtly impressed with the procedure.

"When did you have this surgery?" he asked, deeply suspicious of the miraculous implant.

"I've *never had* any surgery on my leg," Bob explained. There was no reaction from the doctor for a few seconds.

"Well, we, meaning modern medicine, *cannot* do a procedure like this," the doctor began. "Even with lasers it wouldn't work. Besides, your body would have to react to the implant no matter how carefully it was inserted and attached. There would have to be pain to cope

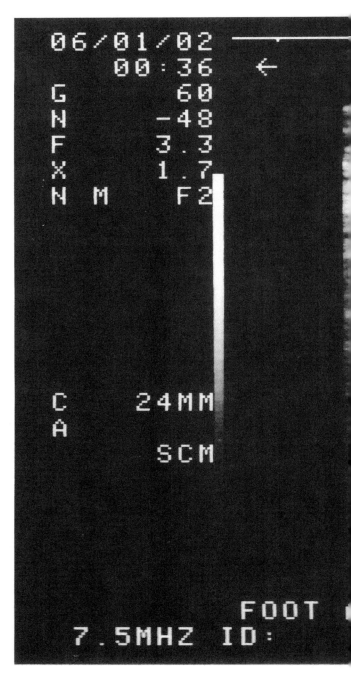

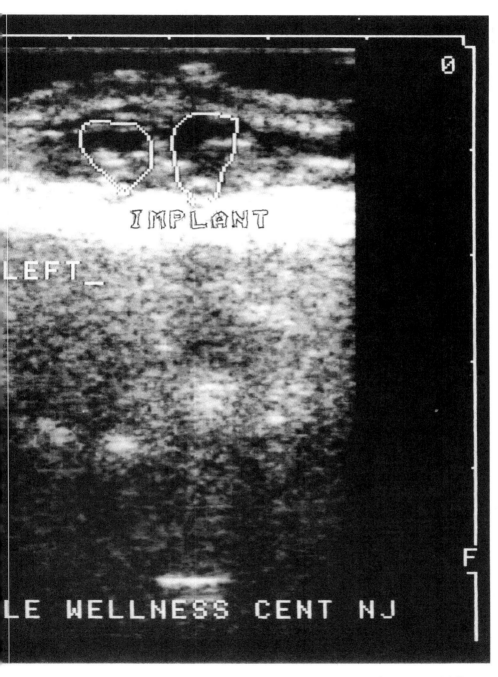

Ultrasound images. Word "Implant" outlined in pen by author for better visibility. However, all labeling originally done by technician or doctor at the medical center.

with, and scar tissue. Usually, there is swelling and discoloration. These are the body's natural reaction to a threat, like an incision."

"I had none of that," Bob said calmly.

"*That's* impossible," remarked the doctor, not so calmly.

Further discussion of the surgery included the possibility of alien intervention, but no conclusions were drawn.

Over the next few years, Bob struggled with the reality of his UFO experiences. Did he imagine or dream them? How would that leave one's sanity, when the bulk of the population said that aliens did not exist?

At his core he knew it *was* real...and he and his left leg were about to get a reminder.

Bob and his girlfriend were at a party one night that was chock full of spiritual healers, Reiki masters, and parapsychologists. The subject of UFOs popped up and Bob mentioned the story of the marks on his leg, which were still visible. He offered a few people

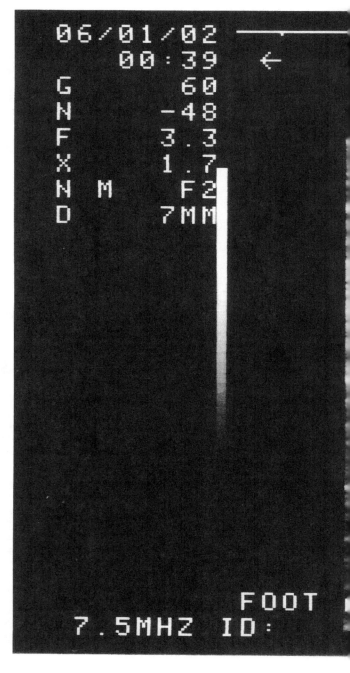

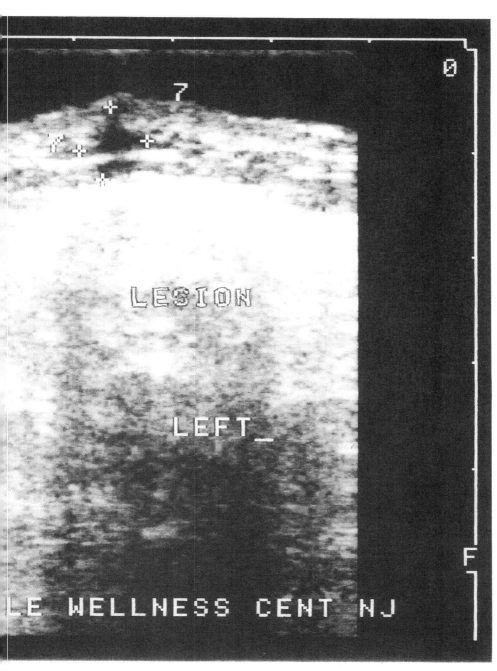

Word "lesion" outlined by author.

a look at the spots hoping they might have some insight into their origins. One of the spiritual folk began sending energy to Bob's leg in an effort to "read" what was going on inside of it. To Bob's puzzlement, he was told that his leg, in general, seemed well, but where the four punctures were, there was a "hole" in his energy field; that is, his own energy was not present in that area. The man commented that he had never seen the likes of that before. Bob asked if he could tell how this had happened, or if he could get a reading from it, and if he could fill the void by psychic healing.

After agreeing to try, Bob, his lady, and the healer moved to a quiet spot in the house. Bob sat on a barstool and rolled up his left pant leg. The man then funneled energy through himself into Bob's leg. This lasted several minutes as the psychic juice poured from the spiritualist into the puncture marks.

Bob's leg grew warm, then hot, in the treated area. He felt a strong

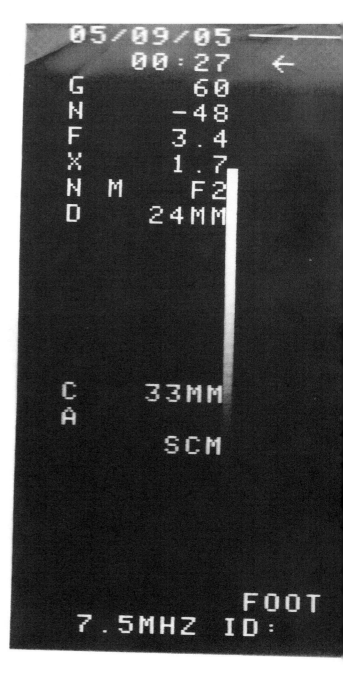

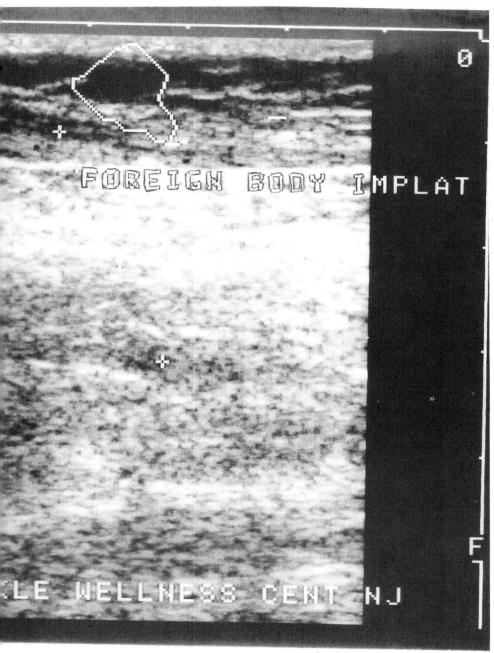

FOREIGN BODY IMPLAT

LE WELLNESS CENT NJ

Wording and circular highlight leave little doubt of medical opinion.
Words outlined by author.

pulling sensation, as if pliers had clamped onto the implant with intent to dislodge it. It was a struggle to keep his leg resting on the chair's lower rim. In fact, he had to hold onto the bar behind him at one point so he wasn't dragged to the floor. This was all done with energy. No one was touching him.

The spiritual man called for help. A lady hurried in from the party room, learned quickly of what was transpiring, and then added her psychic healing abilities to the task. They soon realized that something was trying to suck Bob's consciousness out of his body.

And, strangely enough, each of the spiritualists felt that this was *not* a bad thing. It was not attached to negativity. It was as if Bob was not *supposed* to learn the answer about the implant and that the peculiar void of personal energy around his leg was protecting him from that information. If that was true, great. But what if it was a ruse?

What if the aliens decided to chop off his leg

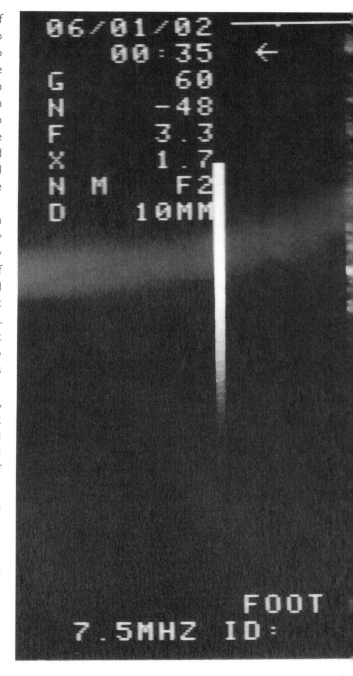

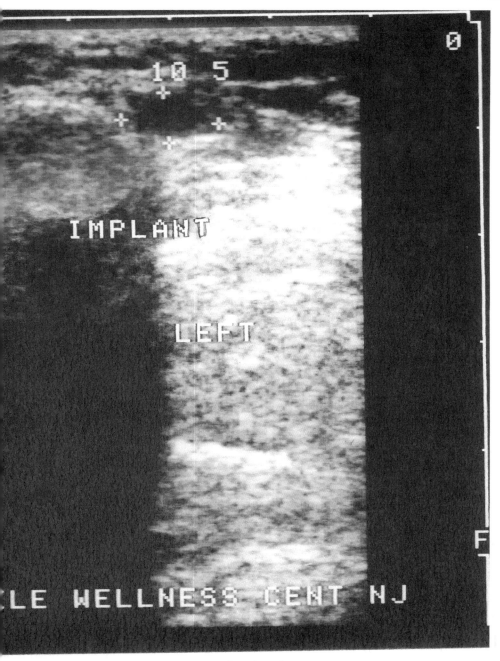

Another view.

in retaliation, or lock him in a dungeon on Mars because he tried to learn the answer of the mystery mark?

At last, with the help of several other spiritualists, Bob's energy was finally grounded. The pulsing surges in his leg subsided, and he was left alone. Those involved, not only Bob and the paranormal helpers working on his leg, but also his skeptical girlfriend, all came to realize the implant in his leg was *real, yet unexplainable* through both *medical and psychic practices.*

That hard-to-believe reality gave Bob a break after the party night and left his life quiet for a few years.

Since the paranormal was quiet, Bob decided to propose to his sweetheart, marry her, and propel them both towards the happily-ever-after ending.

Then in 2009, September, the night before a business trip to Ohio, Bob's dreamscape was awash in memories, things that had no conscious recollection. The scenes were lucid, powerful, and pointed to the terrifying reality of a possible alien abduction.

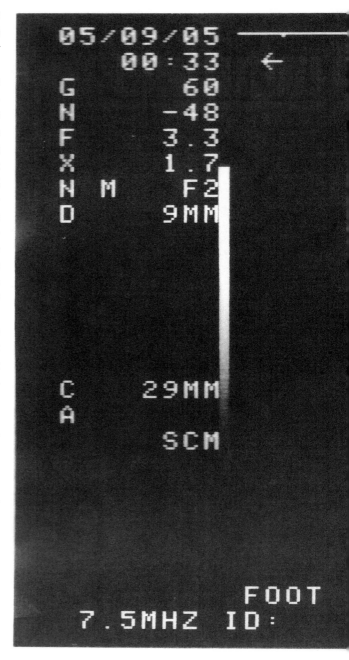

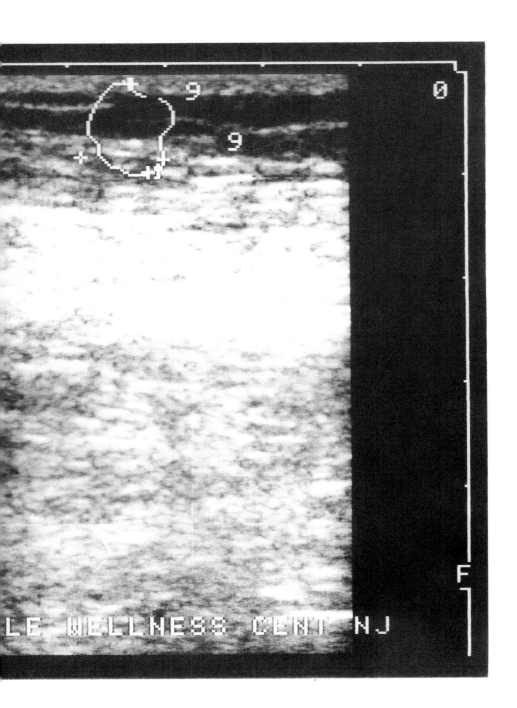

In the memory, he was on a cold, metal table – paralyzed. There was a female presence on the *right* that was familiar, comfortable, but he was unable to turn his head to see who it was.

The table sat in a room that Bob had never seen before. Not far away, he could hear the pitter-patter of naked feet rushing across a hard, smooth floor.

These weird recollections rushed to his conscious mind like the Red Sea upon Pharaoh's army.

Equally fast, it was over.

Bob felt lost. The vibrant dream and its images smacked more of truth than Bob was interested in knowing at the moment. Talking to someone about it would be a huge assist, but to whom? His bride was his first choice, but he believed it best to keep these stories from her, at least in the beginning. Since she was *out to lunch* about the UFO influence on planet Earth anyway, he did not wish to scare her. And he certainly did not want her questioning *his* sanity at this early stage of their romantic commitment.

Startled, uncertain, racked with the unpalatable knowledge that he, like so many, was an abductee, he flew off to Ohio the next morning. On his return, he had decided to share the uncomfortable experience with his wife. After all, if he could not talk to *her*, etc., etc. Though he knew her heart was huge, it would be severely tested by a crazy story of alien abduction. Her judgments, impossible to control Bob knew, would *need* to be released for her own sanity's sake, but would still be painful to *him*. Emotions, however, must remain calm. Temper would be checked. He would remember only his love for her, and that the unearthly conversation about other-worldly kidnapping would be a potential stumbling block to their relationship unless he presented it in his usual clear, logical way. They sat at the kitchen table, coffees in hand. Bob thought hard about his first words.

To his shock, *his wife started the conversation*.

"You're never going to believe this dream I had," she began.

Astonishingly, she went on to unfold a tale of aliens trying to take her with them to some far off place, and she battling against them every inch of the highjack. She remembered them causing her pain for resisting. They poured acid, or something that looked like acid, on her skin to dull her aggressiveness. While the "acid" did no permanent damage, it caused terrible agony. In the end she succumbed.

Bob's jaw hung in the open position longer than was appropriate. He could not believe his non-committal-about-UFOs-wife was describing an abduction scene. He quickly related his near matching experience. His wife further described, while lying on a table in a peculiar room, feeling a male presence to her *left* that felt familiar, known, someone she could trust. It was a mirrored image of Bob's vision and feelings. Originally, they tried to write-off the episode as a shared dream. But a person rarely shares a dream with someone else (see my previous book: *Mid-Atlantic UFOs: High Traffic Area,* Delaware chapter, "The Little Men"). But they quickly concluded the power of the images and the commonality of detail pointed towards some great truth rather than a nightmare.

Bob kept notes on this and many of his experiences. His wife and he communed about the event over and over, capturing new details and clarifying others, like their surroundings, as their recollections multiplied. These additional pieces of the "dream" puzzle fascinated Bob's partner. After all, she was not a student of ufology and was content to ponder the fragments for their own merit.

But Bob was a lifer and had seen more action. Consequently, he was not satisfied with pieces; he wanted the the full picture painted. He decided to be hypnotized to acquire the missing brush strokes.

Bob contacted George Filer, a hypnotist and ufologist from New Jersey, and the owner of "Filer's Files," a UFO information and reporting website. But at their first meeting, Filer warned him, "If you go through this regression, Bob, it is possible that the process may awaken other memories buried deep within you that will come out on their own at a later date. These could possibly be details that you may not want to know."

"I'm okay with that. I want the answers and I want them now."

Bob had never before been hypnotized. He was expecting the pocket watch waved in front of his face, or to stare at a candle flame, or to have to hop on one foot and bark like a dog.

Of course, it was none of that.

The expert quickly and efficiently took Bob to a restful place in his mind. The blinders that prevented him seeing details of his own memories were gradually removed.

Now, he was taken back to the night that he had shared a "dream" with his wife.

There was an alien gray person standing at the foot of their bed. It felt female and that she was "assigned" to Bob.

Immediately he was in another place. A room; he was lying on a table. There was light everywhere, yet no observable light source. A viewing screen was part of one wall with stars spread across it. A powerful thought prevailed in his mind that warned in a friendly way, that he was not permitted to look at the aliens. He was free to move about, however, and to his right was a hallway. Three humans, naked, with blank faces, waited their turns to come into the room.

But time ran out and the hypnotic session was ended.

Bob was disappointed. More detail, he longed for more detail, but it would have to wait.

On returning home he told his wife some of the aspects of his recovered adventure. As he spoke, he could see his lady's eyes glowing from deep inside. She was remembering more specifics from her own abduction.

She recalled being in a type of chair, in a reclined position with a dazzling light above her face. The light was transporting her to the "room," but there was no indication what the room's function was, or where it was located.

Once there, she, too, saw the aliens mulling around and the other bare humans standing outside the room.

In the current time, Bob has found that sharing the abduction experience with his wife has not only brought them closer together, it has cleared his mind. He is good with all that has happened, so much so that he shares his experiences readily with the public, including being a guest speaker at the 2011 Philadelphia MUFON (Mutual UFO Network) Conference. This sharing became a cathartic goal, to minimize dread and augment acceptability with an eye towards learning. More, he feels that relating the stories of his alien encounters, with their *minimal physical effects*,[1] is an important task, one he hopes will open up other people to all the possibilities that wait in our future.[2] His intent is to help others come to terms with what is happening in the world.

In January, 2012, returning home from a business trip in Tulsa, Oklahoma, Bob passed through one of the new TSA obligatory airport X-ray booths. After walking through the machine, he was flagged and pulled aside by security. Bob glanced back at the human image on the screen to see what area of his body was in question. The yellow warning box was displayed on the lower left leg.

The implant is still in place. Some people might claim that since the doctor in Paterson, New Jersey, who examined Bob had an interest in UFOs, that his findings were biased in that direction. On the other hand, any other doctor who tested Bob and was a UFO skeptic, and found "rational" earth-bound-only explanations for his condition, could as easily be said to be biased in *that* direction. It is the gander and goose cliché.

In the end, according to Bob, his life in ufology has unfolded as it was meant.

Endnote

[1]"Minimal physical effects" is well noted. By far, most reports of alien abduction do not support Hollywood-esque scenarios of torture at the hands of the "bad guys." Rather, while the majority of abductees are justifiably frightened by their unknown captors and surroundings, the tests are minimal and usually non-invasive. And the long-term effects are more often mind-expanding rather than crippling. (Read *UFOs Above PA*, Chapter 1: "Deus Ex Machina" for a full-blown example of this.) The same cannot be said for human medicine which has often destroyed a patient's life by malpractices and insufficient testing of drugs before dispensing them to the hapless. During the next TV commercial for the latest "miracle drug," note the long list of horrific possible side-effects, which sometimes include death.

[2]For a comical example of two people seeing the same thing differently, read *UFOs Above PA*, Chapter 16, "Alien Base Camp."

Chapter 2

DOCTOR'S ORDERS
Trenton, Mercer County

"Simplicity is the ultimate sophistication."

—*Leonardo da Vinci*
Italian Renaissance polymath

"Holy smokes, that was no shooting star! What the heck *was* that?"

The night was cloudless and beautiful in early November, 1963, about 5:30 p.m. Doc (real name: Pat Marcattilio, also known as "Dr. UFO") headed home from his job at Allstate Engineering. He pulled into his driveway on South Clinton Avenue in Trenton, parked, and started through the backyard for the kitchen door.

Always a stargazer, Doc glanced towards the twinkling canopy overhead, impressed with its vastness and allure. His passion for the "extra" in life started in fifth grade with astronomy. On many nights throughout the year he escaped to the backyard, lay on the wooden picnic table, and simply watched the stars roll by for hours. Later, as a dad with his own brood, the backyard became classroom as Doc taught the Big Bang Theory, movements of the constellations, and planet composition.

By that November night in 1963, Doc thought he understood the Universe pretty well. Then something caught his eye.

Up in the sky was a big, beautiful bluish-white globe, about three times bigger than any other star, gliding across the sky. It was impossible to determine the object's actual size. Doc was on his patio outside the kitchen and called to his wife to quickly come out and watch this "satellite" streak across the heavens. Mrs. Doc soon pushed past the screen door and joined him.

The newspapers in those days reported the exact times and trajectories that satellites flew around the local atmosphere, so that anyone could go out and observe them. While Doc had not been in the house yet to check the paper for satellite info, he assumed the big light in the sky was the reflecting metal of a human-made device. He did remember that satellites took about twelve minutes to traverse the sky.

Doc and the Mrs. stepped out onto the side lawn to marvel at human ingenuity. After about five minutes, the large, white object had traveled from the horizon to directly overhead, faster than expected. It would seem that President Kennedy's challenge to be on the moon by the end of the decade was well on its way as the object overhead brought them one step closer…

Suddenly, the item took a ninety-degree up-turn and disappeared into higher "space." The object was gone in one second – impossible for a satellite to travel at that speed, not to mention the lunatic ninety-degree turn that *no human vessel could execute*.

"And it wasn't a shooting star, either," Doc confirmed to his slack-jawed partner, as he gently placed two fingers under her chin and closed her gaping mouth.

"What *was* that?" Mrs. Doc practically demanded of husband and Universe. Both were silent.

All through dinner the couple talked excitedly about seeing the white ball, reasoning out all the things it could *not* be, deciding at length that it was one of the darn UFOs that they had heard so much about. They told everybody they knew about seeing it. Some of the listeners became as excited as Doc and his wife to hear the news. Many more, however, listened politely with forced grins.

From that point on Doc's fascination with UFOs intensified. He and his wife began buying books on the subject and studied like it was programed in their genes to do so. They joined NICAP (National Investigations Committee on Aerial Phenomena), a civilian group researching alien activity, and devoured their monthly newsletters. The knowledge-hungry couple wanted to know where, when, why, and who else was seeing unidentified flying objects. Their simple sighting sparked a life-changing transformation from awestruck UFO neophytes to scholars searching for concrete answers.

STRANGE DESSERT
Cape May, Cape May County

Dessert would be impressive.

Doc and his lady finished dinner at the Lobster House Restaurant on Schellengers Landing Road at the Fisherman's Wharf in Cape May. The lady dined on sautéed crabmeat in white wine sauce. Lobster tail with crabmeat stuffing satisfied Doc. It was August 1998, and the nine o'clock sky was beginning to blacken. The couple sauntered across the parking lot, looking for his car, enjoying the cool, salty inhalations of the beautiful, clear summer night.

"Look how big and beautiful the stars are," his lady remarked holding tight to Doc's left arm.

"The whole sky is just plain gorgeous – almost as gorgeous as you." His reply drew out the smile from her lips that he was hoping for.

Suddenly, they saw a large bright shooting star flying across the firmament. The light seemed to be about ten miles high and flew at unknown miles per second. What a delicious finish to a great night of dining, Doc thought.

But the "shooting star" was in big trouble.

It suddenly *stopped in mid-air* directly in front of them.

"What the…" Doc knew that nothing in the realm of conventional aircraft, satellites, or meteors would or could behave that way. It had to be something else.

The couple gazed at the white ball for the longest five seconds of their lives.

And then it *exploded*.

If an understatement could be made, saying the couple was shocked and surprised would be it.

Because…the detonation was *dead silent and bright green in color*!

In seconds, it went from a star shooting across the sky to a huge explosion about the diameter of a penny held at arm's length. Its shape was irregular. The blast of color hung in the sky for a few moments, and then dissipated into nothingness.

Was the object literally destroyed? Did an internal rupture ruin its mass, or had an outside force ended its existence? Was it damaged at all? Maybe it was fireworks. But fireworks did not fly across the entire sky, then stop and hang around before they popped. And they do pop. Fireworks are known for their noise. Yet, there was none. Could the sudden green display have covered the object's departure from our world like a smoke screen?

After their romantic dinner on the wharf, the duo was thrilled to see the impromptu show.

But the drive to their hotel was cloaked in silence. The enormity of the Universe filled the vehicle as the pair contemplated their simplistic existence hounded by complex questions.

TAG-A-LONG
Trenton, Mercer County

Driving south on Route 206 from Trenton on a sunny May day in 2010, Doc held only one cranial concept: errands. If there really are ultra-advance aliens watching us, he thought, why don't they relieve our suffering and end war and disease, or better, the need for shopping?

His comic-socio-philosophical reverie was interrupted by a commercial airliner flying from the west, poking along from the right side of the front windshield. Minutes earlier it had lifted off from Philadelphia International bound for a destination east and coasting about 7,000 feet up.

Doc's glance bounced between watching the racing auto traffic and the airplane. Something told him to keep an eye on it.

Unexpectedly there appeared a bright "sliver" of metal cruising alongside the airplane. He couldn't tell what it was, but he knew it was metallic and that it was flying close to the jet, because the sun bounced off the object differently than it did from the aircraft. For several seconds the metal piece kept pace with the jet.

"What the heck is that?" he thought. In all his studies of UFO phenomena, he had never come across anything quite like this sliver.

As he monitored the situation, something happened to Doc that was out of character. He felt warm and fuzzy; not just Christmas-morning-right-before-opening-the-presents warm and fuzzy, but an increased body temperature coupled with a mild tingling in his chest. Before he could fully grasp his condition, he felt a contact, a mental contact. A message was coming in. A message telling him that the aliens were out there to observe. This signal was for *him*, to let *him* know that they watched everyone in our simple world.

After a few moments the onrush of heated information ceased. The airplane was nearly out-of-sight and the sliver had disappeared. Only the message remained.

SHIP TO SHIP
Atlantic City, Atlantic County

In 1992, Doc and six of his friends were flying home from Key West, Florida. They were over Atlantic City, and the plane would soon begin to turn left and start its approach towards Philadelphia International Airport. Doc had a window seat on the left side of the cabin. The fasten-your-seatbelt sign was on. It was a clear sunny day.

Suddenly, out his window Doc saw a big, bright white, luminescent globe. It was far off in the distance on the left side of the plane, but nearer the ground, estimated to be about 500 feet in the air.

Without warning, it burst towards them in a blur, zooming below the plane from north to south, crossing a large distance in little time, and then instantly returned to the original position in the north.

Doc estimated that the device had flown from approximately New Brunswick in Central Jersey south to Cape May and back again, a round trip of 200 miles, in about four seconds. The size of the ball was impossible for him to estimate, but it had to be big enough to be visible at that great distance. If the estimate was correct, the device was moving at about 3,000 miles per minute, or *180,000 miles an hour!* From that incredible speed, it stopped on a pinhead and flew back in the opposite direction where it again halted in a nanosecond.

For argument's sake, let us assume that the above distance is estimated incorrectly by half. That is, rather than take two seconds to traverse 100 miles, the ball traveled only fifty miles each way.

That is still 90,000 miles per hour! There is no human device capable of that speed in 2014 technology. Nor is there any human on earth who could withstand the rigors of such G-forces during acceleration or deceleration. Nine G-force can kill under certain conditions. It is safe to say there were no humans in that globe unless they figured how to negate the effects of gravity and centrifugal force.

For Doc, this was a phenomenal experience. It was corroborated by one of his friends who also looked out a window in the same direction during the same experience. The two men, co-workers at the local post office, told everyone about the strange flying object, receiving in turn a mixed bag of opinions from "wahoo" to "no way."

While skeptics still outweigh open-minded folk on the UFO issue, the pendulum is steadily swinging towards acceptance of alien existence and the need for disclosure of their intentions. Doc is adamant that the "visitors" come to school our civilization in ways to survive, not only with extraterrestrials, but with terrestrials as well.

According to a study (released on August 23, 2011) authored by researchers Camilo Mora, Derek P. Tittensor, Sina Adl, Alastair G. B. Simpson, and Boris Worm from the United Nations Environment Programme (UNEP), there are 8.7 million different species on *this* planet. This accounts for all life forms. All are worthy and with purpose no matter how simple, and all of them should be considered intelligent. Our ability to fit in with life on Earth has been, and will be, continually tested. Perhaps civilizations from around the Universe withhold *official contact* with humanity due to our poor report card when cohabitating with neighbors on this planet.

Yet Doc's prognosis for a planet-wide awareness of alien visitation is positive. It is happening slowly but certainly. And the numbers of those reporting ET phenomena will continue to rise. So, too, hopefully, will our scorecards.

But first we must realize we are *being* tested so that we can better prepare for the final exam.

Chapter 3

LANTERN EXPRESS
West Deptford, Gloucester County

"It's not denial. I'm just selective about the reality I accept."

—*Bill Watterson*
Syndicated comic strip author and artist
(Calvin and Hobbes 1985-1995)

That Sunday in July 2011, on Dubois Avenue in West Deptford, luxuriated in a beautiful, clear day, and the night promised more.

It was dinner time and Simon and his family were chowing at the backyard picnic table. The barbecue was pumping out burgers and dogs, as was their next door neighbor's, each patio competing for the best smell on the block. Everyone's backyard on that street was edged by a copse of sixty- to seventy-foot evergreen trees that provided wind-break, privacy, and some security – but perhaps, not enough.

After dinner was cleaned-up, Simon's family piled into the house for their evening activities. For some reason, Simon felt compelled to walk to the front of the house. He marched through the living room, straight through the front door, and out onto the porch to look around. It was unlike him to be compelled by odd feelings. Was it a need for watchfulness? Was something wicked this way coming? It was probably nothing. Like a Wild West gunslinger, he leaned up against a post supporting the roof, surveying the residential street, pleased with the pleasant suburban setting as the edginess drained away.

It was now about 8:45 p.m.

Suddenly, something caught his attention. A light appeared in the corner of Simon's left eye that was brighter than the fading day. It was an orange-red glowing lantern/ balloon/thing. It flew from between Simon's house and the neighbor's house to his left. (He'd been competing with this neighbor during dinner as they barbecued.) It drifted smoothly about six to eight feet in the air, working its way at a slow, determined pace. It did *not* make random movements like a balloon or lantern that was being propelled by the wind. Unlike many UFO products, this item *did not* appear instantly from out of nowhere. The balloon must have dropped down somewhere behind the house initially, having missed the huge trees clumped along the rear property lines of the entire suburban block.

Standing on his two-step high porch, Simon gaged the balloon/lantern to be at his eye level. The object floated straight to the sidewalk, made a sharp right turn, moved to directly in front of Simon, and then came to a halt. It was about fifteen feet away.

"What the heck is that?" Simon's logical mind and nuts-and-bolts reality was doing flips and flops over this never-before-seen object.

The "visitor" had a similar appearance to a Chinese lantern (but not exactly), and people had been known to launch them in the area during the summer time for general amusement. But Simon knew exactly what a Chinese lantern looked like and how it behaved. This was not one of them.

This lamp did not have a simple candle burning inside near the bottom. In fact, the bottom of this lantern was sealed closed. Chinese lanterns were open on the bottom to allow access to the candle whose customary flicker could *not* evenly illuminate the entire outside of the bag. But the orange lamp was solid with no apparent seams. It was *not* lighted from the inside like a lantern. Rather, it had a glowing luminescence which seemed to come from the exterior and emanated several inches beyond the object's surface. The glow was uniform around the entire device. Large Chinese lanterns were brighter at the bottom, darker near the top, never uniform.

Despite Simon's rationale that this was not a lantern, his mind would permit no other label.

"What are the chances that a Chinese lantern would float into my backyard, travel around the corner of the house, and stop dead in front of me?" Simon mumbled to himself. Part of his dilemma was that there was no wind that night, nothing to propel the quiet lantern forward, and certainly nothing to bring it to an accurate stop at eye level fifteen feet in front of his face.

To his discomfort, he felt it was looking at him.

Counter to his lifelong experiences with "stuff," this simple odd-shaped balloon felt to Simon like there was intelligence behind it. Not the type of thinking power that he knew had created an airplane, or a baseball, or his front door...That type of intelligence did not accompany the products after they were manufactured. The plane, ball, and door were inert, lifeless, shipped to a retail outlet for purchase, and then forgotten. Simon felt "somebody" was still involved with this lantern in the "here and now."

Perplexed by this uncanny thing, he required reinforcements. He turned to the screened front door and yelled. "Hey, Sweetie, Chuck, come out here, hurry up! There's..." Simon turned back to the check on the object, "...something really weird."

Amazingly, the glowing balloon was no longer in front of his house, but had shot four doors down to the right, which was a distance of about 100 yards, and it had done that in about two seconds time. (That's equivalent to moving one mile in 35.2 seconds, or traveling at 102.2 mph. Remember, the object still had to execute an instant stop at about 100 yards distance. At 100 mph, an average size car with an automatic braking system, including reaction time, takes about 475 feet to make a panic stop. That is about 150 yards, or 1 ½ football fields.) Prior to that, it was moving at a snail's pace. It was still floating at the same height. "What the... How did it get down there so fast?"

Like most families, when dad wants something done in a hurry everyone else usually has something more important to do, no matter how urgent the plea. By the time his thirteen-year-old son had come out the front door to see what the excitement was about, the lantern was moving yet again. The orange balloon was now at the far end of the street, an additional seventy-five yards and was heading upward into the sky off to his left, moving fast.

"Do you see it?" He tugged his offspring off the porch and pointed hard with his right hand, wishing the lantern had not left in a hurry, questioning how it did so. The boy, raised on powerful electronic images, scoffed.

"Yeah, so? It's just an orange balloon isn't it?"

"No, it's not. It's..."

The balloon unexpectedly shot higher into the sky and became a barely perceivable dot. "Did you see that?" Simon was excited now. He hoped that his son got the idea that they were watching something very unusual, something that neither of them, perhaps no one, had ever seen before.

However, hope crashed through the wooden porch floor as the boy noted that it was no big deal and returned to the TV.

An older and wiser Simon charged into the living room, dashed up the steps to the front bedroom and threw up the sash like in a scene from *A Christmas Carol*. Maybe Santa, who, like UFOs, he did not believe in, would whip that orange sucker back to Simon's porch so he could grab and study it. Minimally, he wanted a last and closer look at the strange orange phenomenon that had entertained him for the last ten minutes.

Unlike children's balloons that, once released, will continue to float away on and on until they eventually disappear from sight, this orange device flew to a higher shelf in the sky, but remained visible; it no longer moved.

Simon yelled to his son again to come upstairs to witness the peculiar phenomenon. But junior had little interest in watching a "balloon." He was too old for that. Still, he trudged up the steps to do his father's bidding.

By the time he arrived, however, the orange balloon was gone.

A few moments later, his wife arrived in the room now ready to view the great mystery.

"Never mind, never mind," a frustrated Simon waved her back.

"Come on, Simon, you wanted me to come up. You practically ordered me to see it." His wife moved next to him at the window, but saw nothing unusual. After his brief explanation of the odd goings-on, his lady gave her honest opinion, "Yeah, right."

Simon was disheartened that his family was never going to believe that he had seen something so bizarre and so strange that it was unexplainable in human terms. Why would they? They had not seen it arrive in its spooky manner from the side of the house, and had not seen it come to drill-sergeant-attention directly in front of him. No one saw it bolt from that stand-still to four houses down the street in two seconds. Simon realized no corroboration would be had.

That lack annoyed him. Fully aware that he did not know what the glowing lantern truly was, he was equally aware that he *had seen it* and all its unusual behaviors, *and that it was real*. If nothing else, Simon was certain of his brick-and-mortar observation powers and his sanity. Because of this he also knew that the best results from observing an unusual event was to have additional witnesses. He had half of that, in that his son saw the lantern, though he did not witness its UFO antics. Repeating the story to friends and other family members was risky. He needed the stamp of approval that independent observers would bring, otherwise his credibility would be fried in a cast-iron skepticism. He'd have to keep quiet about a story he was dying to tell.

A couple days later, Simon saw his neighbors, father, mother, and daughter, outside watering the lawn and doing a general overview of their property. Simon thought this to be a good time to find out if they'd seen the orange balloon from a couple nights earlier that passed between their two houses. But he would be guarded on how much info he would divulge. Image was important.

"Hey, folks," he called, giving a slight wave of neighborliness.

"Hello, Simon," the mom replied with a smile.

"Hey, buddy," the dad said with a grin.

"Hey," the daughter spoke in neutral.

"Can I ask you guys something?" Simon wanted an answer but he did not want to seem like a kook. Yet he could not think of any clever way to ask the question other than just ask it.

"By any wild chance, did any of you happen to see that orange balloon a couple nights ago?"

The mother and the daughter quickly glanced at each other, then gave Simon a funny look. The husband right away said, "No we didn't see anything." Then he turned to his daughter and asked, "Did you see anything?"

"Well, yeah I did." The daughter's face was perplexed. "I saw an orange lantern in our backyard. It flew between our two houses and then went out front."

That's when the mom said, "I saw it, too. I thought it was a balloon. But it acted funny."

Neither of them had seen where it had come from. It was just there, coasting from near the trees towards the front of the house. They were not motivated to follow it.

"Why didn't you call your husband and let him know what you were looking at?" Simon was excited. This was the corroboration that he wanted. The daughter even named it an "orange lantern."

He wanted to know more, however. Mom and daughter did not share their experience with the father. Why? Why would people see something unusual and *not* report it to their family members? Would the dad have called them crazy or perhaps made fun of, even belittled them? Were the women unwilling to discuss the unknown, the unexplainable? Were they wary of it? Or was it all simply not that important to a small young family living the abrasively busy, suburban lifestyle? Surely, Simon reasoned, the mom and daughter would have wanted corroboration, too.

But human nature is a funny thing. People don't always do what they think they should. The neighbors' daughter said it best. "I didn't know if I really saw it."

"But you *did* see it. You just *said* so. And *I* saw it, so *you* have proof now that it was real. So do I." Simon was adamant. He wasn't going to let his neighbors get away with any denial program about an object that he himself was sure existed. Relief filled his mind. He could tell his story. Whether folk believed him or not was not so much the point as — he had other witnesses.

The orange device had been mystifying. Simon was not afraid, however. The object made no movements towards him. Yet, he did not try to capture the object for posterity either. Neither were his lady-neighbors alarmed; at least they made no mention of being so. The lantern was only a brief strange consideration.

In hindsight, Simon wished he had gone a few steps closer to see what reaction he could have gleaned from the peculiar lantern. There was no way a balloon or a lantern could sail over sixty-foot trees, drift low at a steep angle to six to eight feet off the ground, and then continue traveling along the sides of the house, make a sharp turn at the corner, all the while maintaining straight lines, and then suddenly gathering enormous energy and fly down the street at amazing speeds. If a balloon dropped in front of the huge evergreens along the rear property line, it had to be low on helium. A lantern, too, would descend after its candle-power had burned or been blown out. Either way, the life of the craft would soon be over and it would not have been nearly as maneuverable as the peculiar orange-red balloon/lantern. The lantern was not mechanized either; there was no motor powering the object around the neighborhood. A motor would have been loud. It would have been a small gasoline engine that would have whirred like a buzz saw. The lantern was silent.

Simon does not believe in UFOs. He does believe in the orange lantern that visited the neighborhood one summer night in 2011. And he has selected to say "that's all he saw."

Chapter 4

THE ROMANTIC RESCUE
Wildwood, Cape May County

"The longing we have to communicate cleanly and directly...is always obstructed by...concern about how our messages will be received."

—David John Moore Cornwell
Pen name John le Carré, British author

Wildwood, New Jersey is known for its wild times for teenagers and for party-people of every decade. September 11, a Saturday night in 1993, was no different for nineteen-year-old Nancy. Yet it was completely different. While the Firemen's Convention after-parties raged along Ocean Avenue and most other streets in the resort town, it was a quiet illuminated metal ball flying all night in the near sky that changed her life forever.

The Firemen's yearly convention was important and fun for Nancy. She belonged to a couple of different firehouses in North Jersey and the seminars always taught her something useful. Award ceremonies, a large part of any convention, gave her appreciation for the valor of others and inspired excellence in her.

It was after lunch when Nancy sashayed onto the hotel room balcony, enjoying the beach and Atlantic Ocean across the street, contemplating which parties she and her two friends should attend that night. Their hotel was on the bayside of Ocean Avenue. Directly across from her was another hotel blocking some of the scenic view, but leaving an ocean vista to the right.

Nancy was peering in that direction when she noticed three large balloons – red, blue and yellow – tied by a string to a railing on the top floor of the hotel property across the street. The second and third balloons were each corded to the top of the one behind it with a two-foot rope. A light breeze kept the three sailing off to the right, angled-up at about forty-five degrees, wavering.

Flying near the balloons, identical in size yet untethered by any string or wire, was a large silver ball, about two feet in diameter. It floated in formation with the three balloons, making it the fourth in line, pretending to be a part of the pack. But it clearly was not, as it remained frozen, as still as portraits in a museum, while its counterparts wobbled gleefully in the soft breeze. The grouping was no more than 200 feet away and Nancy could tell that the silver ball was quite different than the primary-colored inflatables.

She called her two roommates to the balcony.

"Do you girls see that?" Nancy asked, cognizant of the presence of UFOs in our atmosphere on a regular basis, for she was already experienced in seeing them, and fully aware her friends knew of her awareness. She systematically pointed out the difference between the silver ball and the balloons.

"Yes, what the heck is that?" they both inquired. One friend looked her square in the face and asked "What is it with you?"

"I didn't do it," Nancy defended herself with shoulders rising and palms turned upward.

But at nineteen, the wonders of the Universe are no match for the best jeans for going out.

The ladies quickly returned to readying for the convention.

Back in the hotel room before dinner, Nancy checked on the silver ball to see if it remained where she had left it. It did. "What is it *doing* there," she mused inwardly. A simple round silver and unmoving shape, unattached and unaffected by the breeze, there was much to hold her curiosity. Nancy sensed a bothersome strangeness connected to it.

The weather was clear that night, the sky trimmed with stars, harboring only a few remote clouds. With her two friends in tow, Nancy plowed into a party held by the fire company where her old boyfriend was a member. It was about a mile south from her hotel. After the normal cordialities, Nancy and her "former" wandered onto the beach, feeling comfortable, and began discussing the possibilities of getting back together again. He missed her. And she was not sure how much she missed him, but it felt right to be there. After a couple of hours of relationship talk, the young man escorted Nancy back to her hotel.

From the sidewalk in front of her building, she could still see the balloon group.

But where the silver ball had been there was now a bluish-white globe of light hovering in its place. Was this a different object, or had the silver ball "turned on" for the evening? This new development sparked Nancy to tell her ex about the strange object and how it spooked the neighborhood all day long. It was close to 4 a.m.

Suddenly the brightly lit ball started to move.

It flew out to the ocean, about a half-a-mile in a couple of seconds. It zigzagged, eerily coming alive as if from the bidding of an unseen wizard.

Nancy immediately asked her companion, "You see that?"

He watched in silence for about three seconds before the reluctant response, "Yeah, I see it, if you do."

For fifteen minutes they watched with sagging jaws as the globe-light danced solo about the quiet New Jersey sky. Then, unexpectedly, *another* globe shot from overhead in a streak of light and joined the original ball. The two UFOs were identical. The two *observers* thought they had been sucked onto the set of a SyFy Channel Saturday night movie. The aerial dance that the two balls performed flung them through move after move around the heavenly ballroom.

Even at nineteen Nancy was a child of the Universe. She knew there was much more to this world and the physical plane than human eyes could garner. As a supernatural maven, Nancy decided to employ her lifelong gift of telepathy and put the objects in the sky to a test. Strong feelings held that these lights were UFOs and hence backed by intelligence. And she had already experienced other strange flying aircraft, so she *knew* of their existence. A test was in order.

"Do you think I should get back with my boyfriend?" she asked the flying balls from nowhere through telepathically.

For most people, a relationship question might not be a first choice when attempting ET communication. *Who are you, where are you from, how did you get here, or what do you want*, would probably be the headliners. Nancy's question, however, felt right for a nineteen-year-old girl whose major life priority was finding the right man. A giant concrete step towards that goal was poured into a form over the previous six hours as two kids stumbled through carefully placed questions and answers about their future together. The concrete was setting, and the moment of decision was in the balance. If these globes were truly paranormal, truly intelligent, Nancy believed she could expect some kind of physical, or at least telepathic, response.

Suddenly the two objects moved in a peculiar up, down, and diagonal movement. They were synchronized. At first it was not the least bit clear what they were intending, but Nancy and her friend continued to watch. The pattern of quick sharp movements repeated over and over.

Then she recognized it. The objects were forming the letter "N." Nancy had asked a question and got an answer. Should she go back with her ex? The answer appeared to be "no."

Nancy freaked-out in her heart, but outwardly remained smooth. She was used to getting answers in the spirit realm, but getting *direct answers from a UFO* was something new. It was astounding yet it felt important, it felt right, it felt humbling.

Within a few minutes, the globes shot up towards space, vanished in one second and were gone.

In the end, Nancy did not go back with her ex-boyfriend. Good thing. He got married shortly afterwards to someone else he had been dating.

No matter how the Tarot cards are cut or what they say, *that night alien probes saved Nancy's life*. Not by pressing her spirit back into its holding shell from some horrific accident, but by keeping her from making a wrong choice, a choice that would have shoved her along a less optimal path. Everyone knows that the wrong choice can be a longer, slower death.

Nancy felt a touch of fear in the alien globes' easy, quick response to her telepathy. But there was the greater relief that she was not crazy. Another person saw the balls, too. That was corroboration – not mass hysteria as is sometimes claimed by skeptics and the disinformation people from the government. The experience was profound.

One gripe that I and others have about alien intervention is that they don't do enough of it: meaning, it would be nice to have some instant cash appear in my bank account – several million please. The aliens could do that, I think. Send a few electric impulses to my credit union and presto! Or they could deactivate all military weapons, big and small, around the world in one second and end war forever. But they don't.

In Nancy's case, for whatever purpose, the UFOs offered an immediate answer to a complex relationship quandary, and for Nancy's nickel, it was the *right* answer from an unthinkable source.

Chapter 5

GET SHORTIES FROM SOUTH JERSEY

Brief UFO reports courtesy of
The International UFO Museum and Research Center, Roswell, New Mexico;
the National UFO Reporting Center (www.ufocenter.com);
and Filer's Files.com

**January 9, 2012;
approximately 1 a.m.**

Atlantic City, Atlantic County

The three observers were driving home from the Atlantic City airport, and had gone about four miles north on the Garden State Parkway when, suddenly, they noticed a green UFO in the air about 150 feet from the ground. It was moving fast, heading at a slight descending angle. As quickly as it appeared, the vehicle dashed out of view disappearing into the dark sky. There were no clouds to hide it as the night was clear and there were no trees to block it from view. It simply vanished. The observers could not describe the object.

Atlantic City, Atlantic County

As the sun set, the witness stood waiting for friends in a parking lot behind a casino. He happened to gaze upward and noticed three distinct lights moving in a triangular pattern at a constant slow speed, slower than any airplane could fly. His first thought was that it was a craft with regular wings and with an *extra* set of small wings on the nose. But he soon realized that it was not a plane. When his friends arrived he pointed and said, "What is that?" The object was about 700 feet overhead. They looked but none of them could see it. The three lights were visible, but the color of the craft between them was barely a shade darker than the sky above. It was a perfect cloaking camouflage. Then they saw it. One of his friends said *he* had seen the same thing the night before in the area. They were all outdoorsmen, used to facing dangers in the woods, but all of them were scared that night. Soon the extremely large craft moved silently away.

Brick, Ocean County

A solid, pure-white rectangular vessel moved without sound across the sky. Initially it appeared to be stopping, but continued to move slowly. The anomaly looked to be more of a solid cloud than a solid physical form, but there were no clouds in the sky that night. Suddenly, it shot straight up into the air and disappeared. The witness had no recollection of the object being near him at any time during this incident. However, after this event, he discovered a burn on his face and his left arm had been cut. He had no idea how these injuries occurred.

Camden, Camden County

The witness spotted ten UFOs in the air around noon while on Market Street in Camden. They were high above the earth, coming from the direction of South Philadelphia headed northeast. They were all triangle shaped and looked like big arrowheads flying in formation. Eight of them were arranged: two, then four, then two — all at the same altitude. Then the last two flew closer together and lower to the ground. The first six all had a glistening bright chrome color; the last two were a darker metal. Oddly enough, all of these craft together made *no noise*. The witness was astonished by their silence. Planes that land at Philadelphia International Airport make enormous amounts of noise every day.

Delmont, Cumberland County

A prison employee along with various inmates were out in the jail yard at Southern State Correctional Institute around 1300 hours (1 p.m.), when he and the others watched a mushroom/jellyfish-like solid dome, moving across the sky. Although it was high up, it was clearly visible. It was about the size of a football field and the color of dull aluminum. He estimated they observed it for ten to fifteen seconds. The employee claimed that the craft seemed to take energy from its surroundings and then disappeared with a powerful "boom." The sound was like a vacuum's suction. He believed that it was caused from the vehicle breaking the sound barrier. Several minutes after it left the area, two fighter jets began circling the zone where the craft had been. The employee felt that the Air Force must have picked it up on radar and scrambled the jets.

Lumberton, Burlington County

The woman was walking her dog around her property shortly before 9 p.m. Since the area was dark, she carried a powerful spotlight to help guide her way. She became aware of a bright, red-orange fireball in the sky that was about four times the size of Venus. It flew directly over her head, fast and silent, at about 2000 feet and then vanished. Within 10 seconds a second similar object was visible in the north, but was not moving; it was hovering. She called for her daughter to come out and see this strange occurrence, and to bring a camera. She aimed the spotlight on the object as her daughter took pictures. Something told her to flash her light at the anomaly. She did so three times. Immediately the red-orange glow went out, revealing a solid metallic, circular-shaped craft that was rotating counterclockwise. It was about fifty-percent the size of the full moon and was silver in color. It reflected the spotlight beam brightly. The object began to move in a southerly course with no sound and no visible light until it was out of sight. The woman was an avid amateur astronomer with many years of experience and had never seen anything that resembled that object before – certainly not something that would react to signals from a spotlight.

Malaga, Gloucester County

The forty year-old female with her grown son observed what they first believed was a C-5 Galaxy jumbo military transport plane fly over them on Blackwood Road. It was getting dark when the ship appeared just above the tree line. They swiftly realized that the ship was silent, had no green and red navigation lights, and moved too slowly to be a jumbo transport. Next, as the ship flew by, they saw that it had three bluish-white lights and a triangular shape. They pulled into the Comcast parking lot nearby and attempted to take pictures with a phone camera. Suddenly, two F-16 fighters appeared on the scene and the unknown craft evaporated from view. These witnesses came from a family with a military background and were sure of what they observed. Later, when the camera pictures were viewed they showed nothing on the screen. Although the witnesses were sure the large silent UFO was not made by human technology, they never felt threatened.

**September 18, 2011;
approximately 11 p.m.**

Pitman, Gloucester County

While sitting by his backyard fireplace, facing east, the witness noticed a bright white object darting straight down from the heavens going behind some tall evergreens. It was not a smooth decent, but like a wildly fast, bumping gyration. The witness yelled for his neighbors to come out and watch, but no one did. Suddenly, from behind the trees, the light shot back up in a straight ascent and this time it looked *green*. Again, its travel was an uneven, jerky motion. The whole experience lasted about two minutes.

**March 12, 2012;
approximately 7:13 p.m.**

Point Pleasant Beach, Ocean County

The observer was on the telephone while looking outside towards the boardwalk and ocean from his Point Pleasant Beach house. Oddly, there was a bright glowing orb in the sky. Of late, he had noticed more and more strange orbs hovering in the same spots in the sky during evening hours, but this time it was *still daylight*. He grabbed his camera and took a picture as quickly as he could in the hopes of making history. The first shot turned out blurry because he was shaking so much. The second picture needed to be taken as fast as possible. But as he looked through the camera lens to take the picture and then back up, unfortunately, the bright light in the sky had vanished! To his naked eye, the orb had appeared to be egg-shaped and had hovered motionlessly.

Sicklerville, Camden County

As the witness was walking up the stairs in his house, he glanced through the stairway window and saw a bright light. He assumed it was an airplane, since planes often passed overhead en route to Philadelphia International Airport. But this was no airplane. It was a triangle-shaped air vessel with three lights: red, yellow, and white. As the vehicle started to travel faster through the sky, he noticed three stars aligned in a straight line. As the craft moved up towards these stars, they began to shift to his left. A couple of seconds later, the lights, plus the three stars, all disappeared.

Toms River, Ocean County

The observer was driving home when he saw four lights arranged in a cross shape that were blinking in unison in the night sky. The objects moved slowly north along Whitley Beach. Then they started blinking in an alternate pattern; two red lights blinked at one time, and then two white ones. When the witness turned left, north, onto Harding Avenue, they all disappeared. Then they suddenly reappeared. They were still blinking in an odd pattern as the lights began to descend below the tree line adjacent to Toms River High School East. The lights were clearly all the same size and intensity. It could not have been an airplane since a plane would have to fly on its side to make the lights appear anything close to what he viewed. Also, it would have been impossible for a plane to fly below the tree line and go from the ocean, over the bay, over Route 37 and over High School East in that fashion.

Turnersville, Gloucester County

During a snowstorm, the power suddenly went out. The witness had been sitting in her living room chair watching TV. Immediately, out the side window, she saw a glowing, neon-green orb the size of a basketball whizz by the side of the house making a swooshing sound. Within seconds the lights came back on. She geared up to go out, and about ten minutes later went outside to inspect the entire perimeter of her home to determine if there was any damage created by the snowstorm or the orb. All the power lines were connected and in their proper place on the side of the house where the orb was observed. Oddly enough, inside the house only the side where the orb had passed was affected by the electrical disturbances, since only clocks on that side had stopped and had to be reset. The clocks on the *other* side of the house had kept running.

Williamstown, Gloucester County

There was a bright flash from high up in the heavens on November 3. After the flash, a craft was seen by the witness descending fast through the air. The aircraft was a blackish sphere shaped like an aspirin. It moved fast from horizon to horizon until out of sight. While this took place, there were also airplanes flying at altitudes of about 35,000 feet, making condensation trails. The unknown craft was soaring easily two to three times faster than the man-made planes. That same night, the witness saw a small, star-like orb flying slowly to the north. The witness's retired Air Force friend, who had observed all of this with him, said that the flying objects they had observed were of no known origin.

Chapter 6

THE APPOINTMENT

Camden, Camden County

"The supernatural is the natural not yet understood."

—*Elbert Hubbard*
American writer, publisher, philosopher

"C-a-l-l for M-i-ss J-a-smine!" The young bellhop in the red suit with brass buttons and a matching pillbox hat, half sung the words. He had entered the far side of the massive lobby of the Benjamin Franklin Hotel at 8th and Chestnut Streets in Philadelphia, Pennsylvania, and strode across the floor re-singing his address.

As far as Jasmine could tell from people's clothes and the cars on the street, it was about 1930. Her own full-length, peach gown swept lavishly to the floor nearly hiding the shoes that matched her black belt and purse. She occupied a settee behind a large, glass-top coffee table with Art Deco lines on the opposite side of the lobby. She did not know why she should be in the Ben Franklin Hotel when she only lived across the Delaware River in Camden, New Jersey. But there she was, and she would play along.

A fine china cup of Earl Grey was in her right hand. She waived her left at the red suit. "Yoo-hoo," she cooed with her sweetest smile.

The bellhop, and a half-dozen men, turned their attention her way.

"Bellhop," she clarified.

Twelve eyes averted, but the bellhop stayed the course.

"Message for you, Miss Jasmine." The fellow bowed low enough to put the silver tray atop his right hand finger tips within her easy reach. A waft of Brylcreem from the black hair slicked back over his ears filled the air.

"Thank you, young man," her half-smile and twice blinking eyes sent a soft message of kindness with interest. She lifted the cream-colored linen paper from the tray and set down her tea.

"You're welcome, Miss Jasmine. And I'm not that young," the bellhop stood aright with a coy smile and a wink of his own.

Jasmine laughed and waved him away. Playful flirtation quickly changed to deep interest. The note was written in simple block print:

We will meet you in the park tonight.

We? Who is "we?"

The vision ended.

Jasmine was now sitting on the back porch step of her small row house in North Camden. It was a beautiful August day in 1982. Her head was a tad fuzzy as she returned to a normal state following the altered-one. This clairvoyant vision, like so many others she had, was a bit cryptic, but needed to be completely trusted. In her earliest of thirties, Jasmine had long ago learned that second guessing the information she was provided in her visions was imprudent. And this message seemed doubly sincere after arriving on an imaginary silver platter. She would take a stroll in her favorite park that night and let the future unfold.

By 8 p.m., Jasmine glided along the narrow dirt trails and concrete walkways in the North Camden park along the Delaware River across from Petty Island. The night followed the day in nicely, and Jasmine dressed light, but two fashions *up* from a plain walking outfit. You never knew who was watching.

Her attitude was expectant as her eyes dashed around the fields and trees. Something wonderful was going to happen.

She had been hoping for a new boyfriend since she had dumped the last slug a few months ago. Maybe tonight was the night. And maybe "we" meant she would have a choice — every girl's dream.

But after an hour of anticipation and leg movements, nothing happened. And Jasmine noticed that there were less and less people in the park for possible interaction. Where was the "we?"

Suddenly, her attention was yanked skyward.

Five large, bright lights the size of tennis balls at arms-length, with the softness of white incandescent light bulbs, appeared in the sky. Initially, she thought they comprised a giant plane, since she was only a mile or more upriver from the Philadelphia Airport, but the arrangement of the lights was all wrong and there were no green or red hues. They were not in a symmetrical pattern either, but hung loosely together with no metal in between. Also, they hovered in the sky, moving neither forward nor backward, yet quivering like children at a monster movie. She knew planes could not do that.

She wanted to move, but her feet felt bolted to the sidewalk as her knees softened and her heart vibrated like a Max Roach drum solo.

So, this was the "we:" five of them. Strange enough for a brief view, but as the seconds passed, the five lights did not display a need to hurry away. Jasmine's *desire* for the encounter was converting to trepidation.

"I need to get out'a here," Jasmine thought, as fear mounted inside her like the shove of a tectonic plate.

If these lights are the *"we,"* she now became terrified of the *"will meet you"* part. Up to this point in her life, Jasmine had followed her intuitive instructions from her visions. And they had helped her in many ways: finding a close parking spot, timing a request for a raise, and knowing who was on the phone before she answered.

But UFOs were a different prediction altogether.

First exposure to the idea of "aliens" came from the famous 1950's "B" movies at her local childhood theatre. She had believed there were other beings in the universe ever since, even without hard evidence, because it made sense to her. But *"meeting"* these alien balls of light in the darkened park felt far beyond the range of a good idea.

The decision was made for her.

There was a sudden flash in the sky and the five lights were gone.

The sighting had lasted about forty-five seconds, long enough for a good look, so the memory could last for two lifetimes.

Knees firmed, shoes unlocked from the ground, and her racing heart crossed the finish line.

Jasmine started for home.

When she turned the last corner towards the house, her psyche turned its own corner. Something that had been filmy in her mind and heart – whether UFOs were real or not – suddenly washed clear. Their supernatural mystique rinsed away and she was left with a long sighting of glowing spheres in the natural world. The five lights would be forever burnt into her conscious mind, in that fragment of brain matter where the *para* and the *normal* meet, in fulfillment of an appointment made on an imaginary piece of paper.[1]

Endnote

[1] Read another of Jasmine's UFO experiences in *Mid-Atlantic UFOs: High Traffic Area*, Delaware chapter, "The Universe in Her Face."

Chapter 7

EAST AND WEST
Egg Harbor City, Atlantic County

"Calmness is the cradle of power."

—J. G. Holland
19ᵗʰ century American novelist, poet

Suki and Helen had planned for the 2008 Memorial Day evening for ten days. It was not for hotdogs or fireworks that their preparations went into, but rather sending invitations— outlandish lures to mysterious guests.

They were at Suki's cousin's house for the "party" of four. The nice single home sat amongst several atop a slight rise off the corner of W. Clark's Landing Road and Mannheim Avenue, the outskirts of Egg Harbor City. The neighborhood was part of the lowlands overlooking Swan Bay.

Egg Harbor City is smack in the middle of the 1.1 million-acre Pinelands National Reserve, known as the Pine Barrens. In places it is an inhospitable marshy forest undisturbed since pre-colonial times, known for its paranormal connections to the Jersey Devil, strange lights, and hauntings from legendary ghosts like "The Golden Haired Girl" and "The Black Doctor."

The sky that Saturday night was drinking-glass clear. Suki and Helen, members of a New York UFO group, had planned that spring holiday eventide for months. Their goal: *to contact alien beings and ask them to show up in their ships over the skies of the Pine Barrens* – nothing more, nothing less.

Seemingly a brash, excessively ambitious, and ordained-to-fail undertaking, this was, however, not their first time communicating with alien species. Of the five previous attempts, all but one had been successful, and that one misfire was attributed to the buffoonery rather than attentiveness displayed by some of the partakers during their all-night vigil in New York. On the triumphant occasions, small balls of light flashed across the heavens, moved to and fro in clever patterns to signify they were not commonplace craft or straight-line meteors. While these were thrilling at the time, like most humans, the communicative duo was now hoping for more, but not *too much* more.

A surprise awaited them.

The two women had meditated for ten days prior to let the "aliens" know they would be in Egg Harbor City, New Jersey, and that they hoped to see some of their crafts flying around the Pine Barrens. The ten-day meditation was not done as a team but on an individual basis. Suki's request expanded from her Mandala and prayer wheel beliefs; Helen's appeal rose from her cross and holy water background.

Saturday, Memorial Day weekend, between 9 p.m. and 5 a.m. was the communicated time slot, giving a generous eight hours for the ETs to work a fly-by into their late-night schedules.

Around 11 p.m. the duo was on the back deck of the house, scanning the skies. Suki's sister and her husband had slipped into the solitude of their house. They had no interest in sky-watching for undisclosed airborne things. Both Suki and Helen felt good about the night. There had already been a couple sightings of small, brightly lit objects that were not planes or satellites because they jumped, jived, and flailed across the sky in ways no human craft could or would ever want to mimic, confirming their intelligent control by someone *not* human. These UFOs also sealed the success rate of the two watchers as now being five out of six, a notable record in any game.

Then, at exactly 11:30 p.m., looking due east, the ladies witnessed a huge "power-up" in the sky! The circle started out no bigger than any other star, but instantly blew up to the size of the full moon! The color was dull orange with a white halo. A weird side-effect was that all the stars in the surrounding area disappeared, even outside the orange blob. To Suki, it felt that this pop of color manifested far out in space, not in Earth's atmosphere. If so, for it to inflate to the size of a full moon, its diameter must have rivaled entire galaxies or at least a red giant. But unlike those heavenly bodies whose images would have lingered for weeks, the view of the orange ball lasted a tad over two seconds and then quickly vanished.

Helen yelled a "hooray!" An urgent feeling of more to come crept into Suki, and unsure of why, she suggested that they look west for the next occurrence.

The watchers kept their eyes riveted westward. They shifted positions all around the deck, talking constantly, sharing amazements, analyzing the massive, solid orange ball. Certainly, it could have been fireworks. But there were no fireworks occurring in that direction since the night began. It was now past 11:30 p.m. All pyrotechnic displays for the holiday were long over; most ended by 10 p.m. The circle of orange was solid. Fireworks never were. The circle blew up and shrunk from out of nowhere. Fireworks' rockets left a trail as they ascended and then burned out in their designed pattern. The circle came and went in just over two seconds. Fireworks usually lasted longer.

The ladies hoped for more, but were content with the detections received so far. Their meditations had been answered, and each knew they could call it an early and successful night if they chose.

They chose not to.

Both of them had suspicions that more out-of-the-box performances were booked. Suki especially gazed expectantly towards her birthplace of South Korea, feeling that something extraordinary, something that would support the earlier big blast would make itself known.

And at exactly 12:30 a.m., one hour after the first "power up," the exact same display of a two-second massive orange circle with a white perimeter happened again, this time in the western sky, directly opposite from the first display.

They were surprised because they felt that the first show could have been the finale. The thrill that it was *not* was superlative.

Suki and Helen felt loved by those who were creating these displays, since it occurred to the ladies that each was custom made at their behest. They also acknowledged their caring for each other. Firsthand experience of the unknown was shared and corroborated by both women.

Again, they had meditated on a simple physical request: UFOs please come; and they received an astounding physical reply. Their wish was granted. The friends hugged. That night would be memorable for both. If only they could have hugged their alien counterparts to thank them propely for the show – maybe not.

As the night continued, so did the UFOs. A distant light/object (about five miles away) would zig here, and a short while later, another would zag there. Like a tennis match, the objects bounced back and forth, up and down, and then were gone. It was a good night for confirmation of extraterrestrials. By 2 a.m., the UFOs had retired for the night and all was calm.

Suki and Helen retired to their rooms, heads filled with fast lights, other worlds, and their next meeting.

Chapter 8

UFO INVASION OF PRIVACY
Sewell, Gloucester County

"Horror is beyond the reach of psychology."

—Theodor W. Adorno
German sociologist, philosopher, and musicologist

A paradox exploded before the pastor's eyes. With the gleaming metal floating over the house came a blackened fear, as hopes for a future paradise delivered by ET saviors were crushed by the intrusion of a *real alien spaceship*.

It was mid-July 1995 around 10:30 p.m. on Diane Court in Sewell, New Jersey, where Pastor Joe Hornet was visiting his mother. Stars twinkled bright in a clear, astronomer's dream-of-a-night.

Shepherding his Sunday flock was part-time work for Joe. Weekdays, his psychology and counseling degrees helped a different population that jammed his government social worker's office. Joe liked his two jobs because he felt they granted him the bigger picture.

But his view of the world was about to expand a thousand times.

He was at his childhood home discussing with his mother the unsettling contents of Whitley Strieber's new UFO book, *Communion: A True Story*, a tale of alien abduction. Both Joe and his mom had witnessed a massive rectangular UFO in West Virginia skies in 1980.

After several hours of philosophical conjecture about whether ET intentions were noble or treacherous and whether abductions could be justified either way, Joe took his leave, kissed his mother on the cheek, and headed out the front door. With Strieber's paperback in hand, he and his mom had solved the problems of the Universe.

Joe quick-stepped across the front yard to his 1993 Honda Accord parked curbside as he searched pockets for car keys. Suddenly, an unheavenly feeling of something or someone watching him crept under his short-sleeve polo shirt turning his spine to a block of ice. Nothing appeared amiss in front of him or up and down the street. Yet his edginess was intense, as if Jack the Ripper stood by, cloaked in his long-coat gripping a blood-stained knife.

To pacify his uneasiness, the pastor turned swiftly to face the demon-stalker who was no doubt standing between him and his mother's house, prepared to attack.

There was no one.

Instead, what the pastor saw cut through the center of his being down to the core of the planet: a large metallic flying saucer hovered about fifty feet over his mother's house.

Certainty struck him. It was all true. The ship his mother and he saw in 1980 was not a fluke, not a *once-in-a-lifetime*.

Joe's body felt like it had been icebound for a thousand years.

His eyes riveted to the rivet-less ship. It looked to be about fifty feet in diameter, matching the width of the house. Alternating solid green and red lights illuminated the bottom of the craft. It was classic saucer-shaped. The motionless freeze-frame position it held was unlike any hovering Joe had ever seen, and that he knew human ships could not duplicate. Contraptions like the Osprey V-22 tilt-rotor airplane or Black Hawk UH-60 helicopter could not hover without compensating for wind, updraft, downdraft, and every other atmospheric whim. Hence, they were constantly moving. Too, they would be roaring like Thor's thunder at such a close proximity. The aliens were tomb silent. It was the biggest object he had ever seen in the air that low to the ground. It was real and of unfamiliar design.

Momentarily, Joe stepped beyond fear. His look softened. He saw the machine was beautiful in symmetry, seamless, seemingly made from a single piece, display-ready for the Philadelphia Art Museum.

Then the tide of fear reclaimed him. His stomach knotted. It was horrific. It was more than an eavesdropper: it was a threat. It could only be there because the two people in this house only a few moments earlier were passionately speculating on the *yeas and nays* of other-worlder's intentions. The conversation had been animated, electrical. Did the ETs have a tap on the house? Could they know what had been discussed? Was it the topic, the energy, or both that attracted them on a summer night to park over a New Jersey suburban home?

A contradiction popped out of Joe's left brain, headed right, then flopped itself in the middle of both.

He realized this sighting was what he most and least expected. *Least* expected because UFOs were not supposed to appear in full view for anyone; clandestine is their name, and impossible to prove is their camouflage for daily visits. It was *most* expected since the last two hours with Mom brought hopes and ideas that were heart-centered, almost religious, about UFOs. It was their shared, private co-experience from fifteen short years earlier that was as relevant to them then as was tomorrow's breakfast.

The saucer and the minister kept each other under surveillance. Only a few seconds had passed. Its shiny silhouette appeared grayer than the darker sky.

Joe squinted, turned his head away for half a second and looked back, hoping, but not too hard, that it was an illusion, a temporary psychosis that he could reference in an old college textbook. There would be some disappointment, but also relief – and he would be able to sleep tonight.

But the UFO remained. The pastor's mental vessel was receiving batches of awe, shock and fright mixed into his emotional soup.

Now his mind switched to a psychological devil's advocate. What if his imagination could be artificially producing this event, since UFO conversation, dipping into his deepest beliefs and wants, had dominated his psyche for the last two hours? If so, the illusion was powerful. However, he totally dismissed that possibility because he was not making something out of nothing.

House on Diane Court where a saucer confronted the witness from about fifty feet above the roof. *Photo courtesy of Pastor Joe Hornet*

Instead, this UFO was discernible, it was solid, and it had depth and height, and hung in the foreground less than 100 yards away without any visual obstruction between them. There were no strings attached being manipulated by the neighborhood wise guys; nor was it tethered to a construction crane.

The next psychosomatic scenario reared its inquisitive head. This could be no coincidence, since coincidence did not exist. Rather, this sighting seemed personal. Since the entire UFO conversation occurred in his mother's sky-lit family room, this craft could have easily been monitoring their discussion. After all, it is no chore for the CIA, FBI, and other law enforcement groups to capture people's conversations from *900 yards* away using the latest parabolic microphone technology that can be bought on the Internet and parked outside your house, or follow you in a car.[1] How hard would it be for galactic travelers to pick up chat from, say, *900 miles*?

Easy.

Joe glanced at the emblematic giant-eyed alien on the *Communion* book cover then back up at the literal craft. Was this ship manned by intelligent design? Was he being sent a message of undeniable proof, since they floated directly over his childhood home? If so, it would be personal proof only. There were no other people on the street, and no one would believe his story. *Of course*, the object had smarts behind it. It could have nothing less. He suddenly raised the book high overhead for the ship to see.

"Do you look like this?" he screamed in his mind, shaking the book half from disheveled nerves, half from knowing the answer and not wanting it.

No response. The event was starting to get long.

"That darn thing has sat there for at least twenty seconds," Joe reasoned, curious about when the stalemate would end.

And as if to prove its point, as if it had heard that thought, the saucer shot across the western sky a thousand times faster than the fighter jets Pastor Joe had seen two decades earlier at his first air show. The craft zoomed from zero mph to a disappearing blip, covering dozens of miles in a fraction of a second. It traveled like the speed of light, leaving no exhaust trail nor making a peep.

A reality set in that Pastor Joe Hornet was not prepared for. Sheer terror cannot sufficiently describe the depth of his preyed-upon emotions. Scared of driving home alone or being alone at all for that matter, he ran faster than he had ever run in his life, bursting through the front doors of the house that he had calmly left only a moment ago. He slid to his mother's side.

Showing no composure, tears shed his face as his head and hands pinned her bare right arm to the armrest of her favorite lounge chair. The woman was initially shocked to see her noble son broken into despair after only seconds earlier having watched him march out the door in a spiritual assuredness that all was right with the universe. Now he cried wretchedly, inaudibly, crouched on the floor beside her.

After he described the encounter, he prayed and pleaded aloud for God to spare him from this incident ever reoccurring. Twice had been quite enough, three times would be unbearable.

It took over a half an hour of consoling before she calmed and reassured him that he could return safely into the darkness of night to drive home alone. He had never taken a longer journey.

Despite a lifelong interest in ufology, this terrifying experience proved too much for Joe. It was *less* like an eyewitness account and *more* like a haunting invasion of privacy.

He has never seen another UFO since and does not want to.

Endnote

[1] For an actual look at such intrusive surveillance in action, read *UFOs Above PA*, Chapter 7, "The Following," pg. 46. It is a hair- and awareness-raising adventure.

Chapter 9

OF CRYSTAL BALLS AND LAMPS
Glassboro, Gloucester County

"The desire of knowledge, like the thirst of riches, increases ever with the acquisition of it."

—Laurence Sterne
18th century Anglo-Irish novelist and Anglican clergyman

On that October Friday night in 1964 the weather was quiet, and the atmosphere in the empty house, more so. The split level on University Boulevard in Glassboro was perched down the street from Glassboro U. (now Rowan University).

Fourteen-year-old LeAnne sipped her glass of cherry Kool-Aid as she watched ABC's *77 Sunset Strip* on the living room TV. It was about 7:30. From her cushy chair she could see the short five-step staircase that led from outside her mother's bedroom down to the living area. Mom was out shopping and due back soon.

Out of the corner of her left eye, LeAnne saw something move.

"What was that?" her mind demanded in bewilderment. She spun her head around to counter the prickly feeling of being watched. This gave her a partial view into her mother's bedroom.

A glass ball of light, about ten inches in diameter, glowing soft white, flew out of her mother's bedroom about one foot off the floor, to the top of the landing, turned left, and coasted down the steps in an even, self-controlled motion. Inside, the ball was filled with smoke, which swirled about as it drifted downward. It resembled a large bubble. The exterior was thin, like a large globule blown from a water/soap mixture, yet still looking as solid as glass.

LeAnne's insides felt like they were crushed by a rock slide. Fear poured through her near-paralyzed body like molten mercury, deadening every response impulse. Despite the glass ball's lack of aggression, her mind-body-spirit felt the device was created by someone superior, making it a thing of danger. Her thoughts zipped through fourteen years of data to try to identify it. But after the obligatory two seconds of mental searching, she knew no answer was available. Both eye lids then fluttered up and down in rapid-fire like window shades on steroids, hoping to prove that the object was all imagination, or that it was something easy to understand, like a giant soap circle that escaped from the clothes washer. But she knew that was not it. Over and over, she kept asking her mind if she was truly seeing this odd vision.

The bubble was only four feet away. It proceeded to float down the steps slowly. When it reached the bottom of the steps, it gently sank into the floor like a fallen angel and was gone.

"What?!" Her anxiety level reached the ceiling. "How could a ball of glass disappear into the floor without breaking?" she thought as composure returned and she charged to the place on the carpeted floor where the globe had disappeared, rubbing her hand all over it hoping to discover that it was warm or cold or wet or something. She needed to know that it was not magic, but something physical, something tangible, a piece of reality that she could tell her friends about at school the next day. Unfortunately, there was no change in the carpeted surface. It looked and felt exactly as it would have if nothing had happened at all.

But something did happen. The front door swung open. The exhausted look on her mother's face justified the many packages that hung from her fingertips.

LeAnne blurted out about the incident with more excitement than her mother was used to hearing upon returning home from a shopping spree. The normal teenage greeting should have been "hi."

"Mom, I just saw this ball-like glass thing with smoke inside flying down from *your* bedroom and disappeared into the floor in the kitchen." Her mother stopped, the bags cramping her shoulders.

"Really?" The parent scanned around the house, prepared for a prank, or a boyfriend running out the back door. But the house was ungodly still.

"Really, Mom." LeAnne's face radiated deep sincerity in wide-eyed fashion.

"What did it look like?" LeAnne filled in the details about the disappearing crystal ball. Her parent made no judgments about zaniness or overactive thought processes. Mom simply accepted the story and that was that.

The crystal globe never returned.

Many years later, the Glassboro house was sold and her mother moved to North Carolina, while LeAnne found her own place, still in New Jersey.

Everyday LeAnne and her mother talked on the phone.

One day, while locked in conversation, they also happened to be watching the same TV program on the History Channel — a show discussing various types of *orbs* seen around the world. LeAnne was shocked. "Oh my God, Mom, that's what I saw that night in Glassboro. I saw an orb!"

"I remember you telling me about that," her mother said with similar excitement.

From then on LeAnne drooled over anything paranormal including ghosts, orbs, UFOs, dreams, clairvoyance, remote viewing, and much more, while her mother charged into a fervent study of the psychic Edgar Casey.

This "good" experience for LeAnne does carry some regret: why didn't she grab it? Her fourteen year-old's initiative, as precocious as it was, on that night, slumped behind a rampart of fear. Though she didn't know it at the time, the possibility of radiation poisoning, as has befallen a few others who have dared to touch or simply been near alien "stuff," was real.[1] It was better that caution prevailed. But still she believes she should have dashed to the globe and embraced it in her hands and got a feel for what it truly was. She could have poked a finger into it to see if it would pop like a bubble or if it would have bounced off her hand and ricocheted around the room impervious to drywall or lampshades. Today, she is in amused shock over the memory of this event, amazed that such a thing exists, and marvels at the potential assignments it could execute.

Now, if she could only see another one...[2]

Endnotes

[1]See: www.ufocasebook.com/Pineywoods. The Cash-Landrum Incident. On December 29, 1980, in Huffman, Texas, Betty Cash and Vicky Landrum, along with Landrum's seven-year-old grandson, drove through the lonely area known as Piney Woods. There they found a large diamond-shaped UFO hovering over the highway. As they approached the object, Betty stopped the car, and got out to observe the craft. The witnesses noted that the craft gave off tremendous heat. Within seconds of the UFO vanishing, approximately twenty military helicopters arrived, searching for the intruder. After the incident, all three observers suffered from radiation poisoning. Yet, three days earlier, James Penniston, a U.S. Air Force sergeant stationed at RAF Bentwaters, a British air base in southern England used by Americans, on December 26, 1980, watched a small triangle-shaped craft land in Rendlesham Forest outside the base. He actually placed his hand on the ship and said it felt "warm." Afterwards, his only health problem was the mental harassment received from Air Force interrogation, trying to convince him he saw nothing.

[2]For another rare view of "clear glass globes" read *UFOs Above PA*, Chapter 23, "Invasion." The globe's activities in that story, and their consequences, are wildly different.

NIGHT LIGHTS
Kingwood, Hunterdon County

LeAnne, now married, moved into a new house north of Route 12 and Locktown Road in Kingwood, Hunterdon County with her husband and son. It was 1993. The two-story building was surrounded by twenty-two acres of beautiful New Jersey farmlands and, at the time, they were the only family on a quarter-mile stretch of the new road, plopped on the cul-de-sac.

So remote and flat was the property that LeAnne decided not to decorate the windows; there were no blinds or curtains in the house. The family enjoyed the views and could see "visitors" coming from a mile away in most directions. The kitchen windows, pointing northeast, faced a row of trees about quarter-mile across a field (see photos). There was a dual sliding patio door on the left side of the kitchen that led into the backyard. The house was new, bright, and homey, near perfect for the young family, and LeAnne loved it.

One thing was amiss, however, and LeAnne would comment on it *often*. The problem was not about why the air conditioner didn't keep the house cool enough, or why was paint peeling in that one bedroom corner? It was "who put that light up there?"

In that row of trees behind the house, about sixty feet in the air, there was a red light that appeared *every night* for the next two years. The glow resembled a stoplight, except for the red color and its size being about that of a soccer ball.

Initially, she assumed the red ball was on a utility tower or a telephone pole, but a stroll one day across the field to the trees revealed no such human-made structures. A continued look around the trees showed no wiring suspended in the trees and no fixture housing a light.

When the light appeared, it hung about six feet from the top of the tall trees, a good sixty-feet up, no matter what the weather or time of year. It was always in the same spot starting at twilight, but would be gone by dawn.

The peculiarity of the light's presence gnawed at LeAnne's sensibility after that first daylight walk to the trees that found no evidence for it. Instinctively, something told her never to investigate by night. Seemingly innocuous, there was something ominous in its persistence, something alive. And despite dogged efforts, she was unable to get anyone to pay much attention to this light to determine its real story.

"It's just a light, not to be worried about. So why are you?" her husband often responded when LeAnne mentioned the peculiar red globe.

"Because there shouldn't *be* a red light back there. There is no electricity, no power lines. Why would a light be hanging in a tree in the middle of nowhere?"

"There are several private airfields around. Maybe the light is to help guide the private planes…"

"Solberg Airport is more to the east, and its fifteen miles away. They wouldn't put those guide lights that far away from the airport. I doubt a pilot could even see that light from the air. Besides, how many airplanes fly *low* over our house?"

"Well, I mean, I never notice any. But I'm not here all day."

"Well, I *am* here all day and they *never* do."

The line of trees was over a mile from the nearest street. Pittstown Road, northeast of the tree line, which ran north and south, was the next available area to have power lines running along its length. But there were no lights along Pittstown Road. So the chance to confuse them with the single red light hanging high in the trees was non-existent.

The most disquieting aspect of the red light was that it was there *every single night*. It arrived at dusk and stayed until dawn, yet its exact arrival/departure times were never witnessed. LeAnne did check on the light almost nightly over the two-year period at various times during the evening to see if it was there. Every late-night bathroom visit was accompanied by a glance out a nearby window in the back of the house to see if the light was in fact shining true. It was. On plenty of evenings, LeAnne was up to two or three o'clock in the morning talking with her mother about a variety of subjects. The one subject that always arose was the red light.

"Mom, that stupid light is out there again tonight. I wish I had a good reason why it was there, but I don't. Every night the darn thing shows up again and again and again. It frustrates me. I wish it would leave."

It was a two-year-long mystery.

But when adjacent properties were sold for new housing, the red light vanished. Never again was it seen anywhere in the neighborhood.

With that problem solved, the next problem arose: a *white* light.

LeAnne noticed this new glow on the first night she realized the red nuisance was gone.

This light was at a greater distance and a more northerly direction than where the red one had been, but exactly how far she could not estimate. It was not a star or a planet or a satellite; this she was sure. It *did* resemble a helicopter light. The problem was that there was no reason for a helicopter to fly over the exact same spot near the horizon several nights a week for hours at a time. Also, she could hear no noise from it.

The white light glowed over many years.

Her son grew up with the light being present in the sky and present in family conversation, and eventually he took it for granted. But when he initially saw it as a small boy, he was upset.

Trees behind the house in Kingwood.

Far tree in the center is the one that held the mysterious red light.

"Mom, there's a light outside my bedroom window and it bothers me. It's always in the same spot. There's *something wrong* about it. *It's stares at me every night.* Do you know what it is, Mom?"

She could not honestly tell him the answer, but she knew exactly what he meant about it "feeling wrong." Determination grew in her ten-fold. LeAnne's "mom" defenses kicked in, and she decided to find the source of the disturbing flicker.

Searching out the electrical menace became a priority. A dozen times LeAnne blasted her auto around local roads at night to find a path to the white light. Once found, an explanation would be had and her household would be settled on the matter.

But none of the few country roads took her to the light's location and she could not even see the culprit from any other position other than the back of her house. So the search became an enigma about its exact location and a conundrum on how to get there.

Obviously, the roads did not go far enough into the woods to get her to the trees where the light was approximated. She did learn that there was no power supply heading back towards that desolate area from any of the streets she had been on.

Several questions perplex her: If the light is human-made, why is it not on all the time? If it is a helicopter, why would it shine in one location hour after hour and never move? What is the point of putting a light in the middle of nowhere in the first place? How could she only see it from her property and not from other surrounding areas?

The light still appears occasionally. While less of an annoyance, it still shines as a bright question mark that LeAnne thirsts to answer.

Chapter 10

SILENT DIVE
Bayville, Ocean County

"Every doorway...has a story."

—Katherine Dunn
Novelist, journalist, radio personality

Paranormal archaeology is the attempt to determine if spirit activity is attached to particular structures, sites, and/or artifacts. David, a three-time book author on the subject, had seen his share of badly behaved bed and breakfasts, the dead rising from seaside sands, and haunted Nazi Lugers. He had over his lifetime grown comfortable with the ghostly unnerving.

UFOs were another matter. Curious about their reality and potential impact on society, David maintained only a peripheral concern that, perhaps one day, he would elevate to a higher priority. But his spectral studies kept him busy aplenty and his desire to expand into other realms could wait.

That was the plan.

However, the best plans are often devastated by powers far over our heads. And in late June of 1995 David's plans would plummet to the drink.

He was driving his black Chrysler New Yorker from downtown Bayville along Veeder Lane toward his home on Windjammer Court. "The Lagoons" development was his home, a human-made neighborhood of streets, houses, and docks built on the western waters of Barnegat Bay. His errands completed at the local grocery store, he was eager for a quiet night of TV and ice tea.

It was close to 9 p.m. A windless dusk with clear conditions and few clouds set the sky with a pinkish afterglow.

Rolling east along Veeder Lane, he was still several blocks from the first street in his development, Moorage Avenue.

Suddenly, from the corner of his left eye, a bright flash of light appeared high in the sky. It was round and glowing pure white. Its size was similar to a full moon, making it a huge piece of construction, and it descended at approximately a thirty-five-degree angle at a constant, high speed but without a contrail. With his driver's side window down, David fully expected to hear an ear-aching roar from the charging ball, but all was summer-night quiet.

At first, David feared the object was going to crash into one of the roofs of his neighborhood, maybe even his own! As the circle rocketed ever closer, he stomped the Chrysler to a halt and waited for the disastrous impact. If it hit a house, at least he could be one of the first on the scene to lend assistance. But as the solid ball raced towards the homes, it *slowed* as it passed over the house tops of Moorage and Ocean Gate Avenues before noiselessly dipping into the eighty-foot-wide canal waters between Storm Jib Court and Spinnaker Court.

He assumed.

Because of his proximity, the buildings on Storm Jib Court blocked his view of the object hitting the water.

Why was there no "boom," no crash, not even a large splash with accompanying fountain of bay water erupting like "old faithful." Despite the object having throttled-back during the last 200 feet of descent, the speed was still momentous and any solid object of that size would have caused a voluminous splash. But the streets were calm as if grouped in meditation.

To his best observations, David guessed the bright white ball had hit somewhere behind the second or third houses on Storm Jib Court. With excitement over the wild phenomenon, and the liberation from concern about a crash, his investigative know-how stepped up to try to find some answers.

Onto Storm Jib Court he motored and parked across the street from the suspected landing area. Darting up and down the street, he looked hard into the backyards and docks of the cute single houses, searching for signs that a large, round circle had banged into the canal, leaving some form of residual evidence. But none was visible.

David debated for a quarter of a second on whether he should knock on someone's door. To an investigator, answers were everything. Having just seen one of the more inexplicable anomalies of his life, the need for information screamed loud in his head. To knock on a stranger's door, which offered a scant inconvenience, carried a small price tag considering the owner may have had a closer look at the object.

Only three knocks brought a swift opening of the warm red front door. For most other people, starting a conversation about bizarre paranormal activity with a stranger might present some anxiety. Despite David's ghost hunter's interviewing expertise, discussing UFOs was all new. And while his inner drive for answers shoved him to the door, he knew his mind and mouth would need to do improv.

"I'm sorry to bother you. I'm David from Windjammer Court," he started basically as an attractive younger couple opened the entrance.

"What can I do for you?" the man asked, shaking David's shaky hand.

"You may or may not believe this, but I just saw a giant white globe fly through the sky and hit the canal right behind your house. I was wondering if you guys had witnessed it."

The couple turned to each other with looks that bespoke Halloween madness, asylum commitment, and practical jokes all in one second. They quickly turned back to David, but looked past him for co-conspirators.

"No," the woman of matching brown eyes and hair said nicely. "Everything is quiet around here."

"This thing was moving fast, and had to be fifteen to twenty feet in diameter." David felt that he was now more salesman than detective. He truly wanted someone else to have seen the unearthly object. Though the years had taught him to trust his senses even when stretched by unearthly visions, it was always better to have another witness for substantiation on an incident. "May I ask...were either of you in the back part of your house or on the dock in the last five minutes?"

"No we weren't," the man answered, though David could see his eyes were already glazing from falling interest. And he knew the Q & A session was over.

"Okay. Well, thanks anyway. Sorry to bother you." He shook hands again and started down the walkway. He wasn't sure if he had heard snickering as he crossed the street to the black Chrysler.

David's exposure to a blazing facet of the UFO saga burned the reality of out-worlder possibilities on his open mind. He would never look at the sky the same way. Actually, during short or long trips from the house he constantly monitors the skies, testing alien veracity, egging them to "do another trick." Seeing a UFO once is riveting, yet incomplete. It opens the flood-gate of imagination, but the river of information holds itself back. It is like having a Japanese appetizer: it is the first portion of a vastly greater meal, but it does not satisfy. It makes you hungrier for what is to come.

The 1995 sighting was not frightening to David. UFOs were things he had often thought about, yet never wished for. Perhaps his friends in the spirit realm got the ear of an alien big shot and suggested David as a good candidate to impress with a falling sphere. Maybe his maturity had reached a level that captured alien interest and they decided to throw something his way to watch his reaction, a trial before advancement into the fraternity.

The blatant truth is we don't know what the aliens' motivations are unless we ask them. Then we must hope the answer would be understandable and honest, something that could be built upon in our current time. Having answers would be "wahoo," but if these answers had no immediate effect and would not until the distant future, say a thousand years from now, then what is the point for our fretting over deep social upheaval or world destruction by the aliens? Governments and religions would be business as usual while the gradual acceptance of the visitors as reality would seep into human consciousness.

Perhaps a ball diving into water without producing the second half of causality was a glance into the Reality's trap door.

NORTH JERSEY

Chapter 11

HEAD-ON
Burlington Township, Burlington County

"Trust not too much to appearances."

—Virgil
Ancient Roman poet

Louie was sure of it; *two commercial airliners were about to collide!*

Louie, a Jersey resident, worked at the U.S. Steel factory south of Morrisville, Pennsylvania, directly across the Delaware River from Bordentown, New Jersey. It had been busy at the plant. Manufacturing was up almost ten percent[1] and the work atmosphere was buzzing due to management pressure and employee-team pride.

On the property there were signs everywhere for the four directions: north, south, east, and west. This was important for crane operators moving massive pieces of steel throughout the plant. Because of this, Louie's sense of direction was acutely clear while he was at work.

It was March 23, 2013, a Saturday evening at about 6:45 and, after staring at chunks of steel all day, he felt that he needed to soften his outlook with a glance at nature. He walked away from the radiating steel operation to watch the sunset. The sun had just rested behind the furthest building on the property, a long, low one-story building, and though the sun was gone, its aura burst from behind the structure like a movie's happy ending, keeping the sky and its few clouds well lit.

Then something caught Louie's eye in the southwest.

That area of the sky was frequented by local commercial aircraft as part of their travel route in and out of Philadelphia International Airport. One airliner was visible flying from the southwest headed for Louie's position, another one was moving from the northeast, both leaving contrails making their progress easy to track. They were headed towards each other on parallel lines, which Louie could see left them plenty of space by which to pass each other, but less than he expected from FAA regulations, which he didn't know. Their altitude was around 20,000 feet and visibility excellent.

Suddenly, the plane from the southwest made a sharp left-hand turn, aiming it at the oncoming craft, putting the two planes in jeopardy of a collision.

Louie's intestines tried to climb out of his ribcage. His jaw unhinged and nearly fell off his face. He expected a fireball explosion any moment as he reached for his cell phone and readied to dial 9-1-1. Even though the disaster would be over his home state (Burlington Township), the Pennsylvania authorities would get the search-and-rescue ball spinning. For some reason, the northeast plane made no adjustment in trajectory, but barreled ahead in an insane game of "chicken."

With his attention welded on the two planes, Louie never dreamt that the situation could become any more intense.

But it did when something unexpected popped into the mix.

From nowhere, a gray circular dot manifested in the sky like a magician's trick. It looked to be twice the size of the jet airliners. The gray ball hovered motionless, about 200 feet directly above where the two planes looked like they would intersect.

"What the heck is that?" Louie questioned inside his head.

He held his phone and his breath. The two planes crossed paths, contrails marking their way, the southwest plane precipitously close to the other, no more than a half-dozen plane-lengths. That would have to be considered a near-miss considering airliner speeds of 300-400 mph.

But there was no collision. The southwest plane straightened its course and continued northward as if nothing had happened. Though, certainly, the cockpit conversation between the pilots of each plane and with the local air traffic controllers must have been legendary.

Under normal circumstances, airport towers instruct pilots to keep minimum distances away from any other air traffic for safety's sake. So, to make a wild left-hand turn into the flight path of another passenger airliner, jeopardizing many lives in both planes, would require an FAA investigation with possible fines for the operating airline, and a possible temporary or permanent removal of the offending pilot's certification. Such a turn would only happen if something went terribly wrong inside the cockpit. Even if the southwest plane was off course, a correction *after* he passed the oncoming jet would have been easy. From Louie's perspective, these two planes looked to be dangerously close together from the outset. Perhaps instrument malfunction, pilot error, or both was the answer.

After the airliners passed safely by, the gray UFO tilted towards Louie's position and, as it did, there was a bright silver flash, which was either a reflection from the final rays of the sun, or maybe a surge of energy from within the circle itself. It then dipped further down towards the contrails and vanished. The entire scenario had lasted about three minutes.

The classic question dove into Louie's mind: did the appearance of the gray UFO *prevent* a mid-air collision, or did it try to *cause* a destructive impact between the two craft?

Louie pondered the miracle that he had witnessed as he studied the southwest plane casually sailing northward over his head. He had a great story to tell his co-workers.

But it would have to wait. Within a few minutes, more aeronautic strangeness began to unfold.

As he saw the southwest craft leaving the scene towards the northeast, five large jet planes plowed into the area *from* the northeast, flying in tight formation, abreast in a single line, with the center plane slightly in the lead. While Louie felt that they were commercial airplanes due to their size, their flight behavior was anything but. *Commercial jet liners do not fly in tight formation.*[2] Possibly, these were jets from a local airbase, probably McGuire, though definitely not jet *fighters*, which are often dispersed by the Air Force when UFOs are picked up on radar.[3] However, the three-minute duration of the sighting was not enough time to scramble even the fastest Air Force interceptors, let alone large cargo/bomber/radar aircraft. These planes were already in the air when the previous incident occurred. Unless, of course, the gray circle had appeared elsewhere prior to Louie's seeing it, and had been picked up on radar by the Air Force. But even with that, why would the military send bulky, slow-moving bomber-sized craft rather than interceptors?

As Louie scratched his head through question after question, the magic returned.

Suddenly, the gray circular object appeared once again in the heavens, a couple miles directly in front of the lead plane.

Once again, Louie was concerned about a head-on collision – this time between the circular gray object and the lead jet. His heart picked up the pace of a runner at the finish line.

But while still at some distance, the gray object suddenly...was gone again, and the five big planes zoomed southwestward maintaining their formation all the way. This segment lasted about two minutes.

Being the weekend before Easter, perhaps the five planes *were* commercial flights, Louie thought. But commercial flights *are not permitted* to fly in formation; only military craft do that, with the occasional exception of airshow performers and private pilots. And there were no airshows performing anywhere near that area of sky at the time.

Louie was amazed and happy that there was no mid-air collision. He was also wowed by two large gray spheres or circles (or the same one *twice*) coming and going as they/it pleased. It has brought him full into the alien story and its potential consequences upon life on Earth. Now that they are here, he muses, what's next?

One thing they were *not* doing. They were *not* studying airplane crashes or near misses. *We* do that. If we do it, it is safe to say "they" *do not do it.* They have already *done* it with their own "planes" millennia, eras, or eons ago. Being the causing force in an airliner mid-air collision would teach them – what? What information could they possibly garner from an alien-made tragedy that they could *not* get from all *the human-made tragedies that play out every day* somewhere around the world? Surely, the UFO was there either as a neutral observer or as a preventative.

Successful human-ET cooperation would require our trust in their incalculable intelligence, their inestimable experiences, and whatever accompanying wisdom that might ooze forth from the combination of both. When it comes to intra- and intergalactic anything, we are the students – not the instructors – sitting in the back row of a Universe-long classroom.

Endnotes

[1]According to the International Trade Administration, Department of Commerce:
- From February to March 2013, U.S. imports and exports of steel mill products increased 2.5% and 6.1%, respectively.
- U.S. steel production increased by 9.6% to 7.3 million metric tons in March 2013.

[2]This is not to be confused with The Stanford Aircraft Aerodynamics and Design Group's 2008 proposal that commercial aircraft, flying in formation, at from two- to five-miles distance between planes, (front to rear, *not* side-by-side as in the above story) can reduce fuel consumption by as much as twelve-percent. As of June, 2013, this has not been approved since FAA regulation "14 CFR 91.111" still states:

Operating near other aircraft.

(a) No person may operate an aircraft so close to another aircraft as to create a collision hazard.
(b) No person may operate an aircraft in formation flight except by arrangement with the pilot in command of each aircraft in the formation.
(c) *No person may operate an aircraft, carrying passengers for hire, in formation flight.*

[3]See *UFOs Above PA*, chapter: "Media Disc."

Chapter 12

GOD'S COUNTRY
Hackettstown, Warren County

"No one is so brave that he is not disturbed by something unexpected."

—*Julius Caesar*
Roman Emperor

"What the hell do they think they're doing to me!" Jake took his plate of partially eaten ham-and-cheese on rye and sailed it across the room, smashing it into the refrigerator. A million white ceramic pieces shattered to the floor along with clumps of dead sandwich.

Jake was alone at his kitchen table. He shoved his face into his hands and squeezed his fingers through his hair front to back, hoping to rip out the inevitability of being laid off. He just opened the company letter that arrived in the mail that Saturday morning, confirming Friday's verbal shock. Due to an unforeseen slowdown, his eleven years of experience were no longer needed at the North Jersey department store. The customer service department would have to get along without their top supervisor. Four years at NYU wasted.

It was May 2003, and there were plenty of other jobs around, but Jake had really enjoyed working at the national chain store. He knew everybody there; he liked them and they liked him. Now, not only was his weekend destroyed by the grind of upgrading his resume and reading through the want ads, but also from the sickening feeling that he would once again have to do something that he hated: he was going to have to be interviewed. While Jake was the master of solving retail problems in line with corporate policy, as well as seat-of-the-pants techniques, doing interviews was his worst nightmare.

His stomach was already starting to tighten.

But Jake was a religious man. He decided to call on divine inspiration and seek guidance. He pushed his depressed self into the backyard and sat on a porch chair. As he gazed to the heavens, he began to pray.

An answer came in the queerest of ways.

At first Jake was afraid. He had wanted his prayer answered, true, but he had not expected God to send a physical anomaly to hand-deliver the response.

An object suddenly appeared in the sky over Jake's backyard. It came from the southeast and hovered close overhead. Initially, he thought the UFO was a large plastic bag floating above at close range. But a second after seeing it he knew that conclusion was *way off.*

It was a giant circle that looked like a colossal blood cell. It had a red rim and a black center and was as big as a small house. Its surface was like wavy water. It sat only thirty-feet above him and had no insignias or markings to show it was a commercial or government venture of any kind. The whole thing made no sound.

Man and "amoeba" stared at each other for twelve minutes, a virtual lifetime of sitting still and wonderment. Then it flew away in a northeastern direction at tremendous speed, something Jake could not calculate. It was unlike anything he had ever seen before.

Was it a miracle? Was his prayer answered?

Perhaps in some way it was. While the UFO did not drop off a job application for Jake to fill out, it did confirm one of his heart-felt *beliefs* and turned it into a solid chunk of *knowing.*

He always believed in the Bible and always believed in UFOs. Some of them, he feels, are good, some are less so.

That day in May 2003, Jake believed that God sent that UFO to see him. It was a good one. And it did answer his deeper prayer; it made him feel better. It also made him a braver man because he has found the courage to share his story with others, despite the potential for ridicule.

This event changed his views on alien aircraft. Never again would he consider them invaders, trespassers, space-brothers, or just curious travelers.

They are sons and daughters of the divine.

Two days after the event, he found a job.

Jake spends a lot more time now praying in the backyard.

Chapter 13

CHARACTER SKETCH
Paterson, Passaic County

"Good breeding consists in concealing how much we think of ourselves and how little we think of the other person."

—Mark Twain
American author and humorist

Mary used to date Mikael. She does not date him any longer; wrong choice. It was too hard for them to find common ground. And while she wishes him peace and contentment, he will probably never find it. Here is Mary's story of her friend.

Mikael was born on January 1, 1990, in Laolao, Saipan, to a mother who was a third generation Japanese native of the island, and to a U.S. Army officer-father who was stationed in the Pacific.

One of the Mariana Islands, Saipan is a place as remote as it is unfamiliar. The fifteen-island grouping lies in Southeast Asia, due south of Japan and east of the Philippines. Water isolates the small isles for over a thousand miles in every direction.

The newborn was not destined to play amongst tropical Asian islands, however. His parents perhaps felt that he would not fit in there. He was too different.

After his birth, the family moved to heavily populated, all-American Paterson, New Jersey, in the fall of 1990. Once in the "melting pot" population it was hoped that Mikael would meld into the mix.

His father was a loving man, strong, assertive with a touch of humor, and the disciplinarian. His worse drawback during Mikael's early years was that he was never around. The U.S. Army kept him hopping. His mother was a light-hearted, live and let live, simple lady. Her Buddhism was followed religiously, even though her son found no interest in it. She adored her son and his two-year younger sister, taught them by example rather than lecture, but bowed in deference to her husband's decisions about the children's proper life choices in a modern world. That is: follow the leader. Do what everyone else does. Study hard in school, get your masters and a job in a growth industry, and you will be happy.

Mikael dove into this box and enjoyed it for as long as he could. Eventually, like for many, the box wore out, broke apart, and was discarded. Bigger boxes were tried, but in the end, Mikael was not content with pretend ideas with a cardboard façade. His memories would not allow it.

Mikael remembered aliens visiting his bedroom every couple of nights when he was between two and five years. He remembered them as tall and humanoid in looks, blonde-haired, blue-eyed and generally pleasant in demeanor.

Unlike many reports of alien visitation, Mikael was allowed to keep his conscious memory of these visits. The only thing that was hidden, as far as he could tell, was the information that they shared during their "teachings."

The strangers would physically wake him from sleep, tell him to put on his little coat before they walked him outside onto the driveway at the back of the house, and lectured him – never once witnessed by sleeping parents or neighbors. When the "talk" was over, they escorted him back to his room, made sure his coat was hung up, and that he was tucked into bed. Mikael never saw them come or knew how they left.

The specifics of those coveted conversations were long forgotten, but the *lessons*, the true meanings of the exchanges Mikael felt were imbedded deep in his psyche. Their impact, he knew, had not and would not surprisingly burst forth like a flowery blossom in a time-lapse video, to display some tidbit of alien genius during an emergency. Rather, the lessons were part of who he was, and expedited who he was to become. He even remembered the aliens holding his baby sister in the latter part of his three-year schooling. Did they impart lessons to her? He did not know. This part of his life was so sacred to him that he would never discuss it with his sister, even in later years. But he felt these were the good times with the good aliens.

But Yin and Yang comprise all things, including beings from far-off places. Mikael would soon experience the darker side of the schoolmasters.

One time, beings came to visit him, but the process was different from the casual stroll on the property. They took him to a different room. It half felt like his bedroom, and half not. He had no idea where it was or how he got there. After arriving, he was told he could take a piece of candy out of a box. Mikael hurried to it with innocent delight. Finally, a reward was coming for all the interrupted nights of sleep and for enduring lecture upon lecture, meaningful as they were.

His right hand took the dive into the carton. But the four sides of the "box" suddenly collapsed on his hand with a firm, irreversible grip. Mikael's hair stood on end. The box would not release. While the grip did not hurt, he was afraid of the ominous restraint. But yanking and pushing did no good; he was locked in.

His eyes darted about for help. There was none. He cried, feeling trapped, suddenly missing his parents and sister, missing his bed and favorite teddy bear. His little body rattled like a coppery beech leaf in a January wind.

Then he was probed.

This moment of terror and violation was a black memory for young Mikael. The recollection sent shivers through his bones and dogged many of his early dreams. Yet, with time he had come to consider it nothing more than a medical exam, akin to a temperature reading with a rectal thermometer. He knew that his fear of the unknown made the event thirty times more dramatic than its reality, and he would always concede that the terror was from how the exam was begun, not by the exam itself.

Subsequent visitations by the humanoids reverted to the teacher/student, lecture/lesson pattern without physical exams. But Mikael would never be quite so trusting again.

Then, as if in celebration of a mystical graduation, the lessons stopped.

Mikael had no remembrances of visitations during his later childhood or teenage years. And perhaps, like a graduation, the information had been imparted, school was closed, and it was now up to the student to survive or sink, using or not using the shared info as he saw fit. And, like most teenagers, he chose not to use it during those lunatic, pre-twenty years.

Despite efforts to bury his out-of-world experiences in the backyard of his mind under a compost of social disapproval, it was never truly forgotten. He received regular reminders of his E.T. studies on a daily basis from the people around him, in a way that perplexed and infuriated him. It was in the way people looked at him.

Wherever he went, one quality of Mikael drew curiosity from casual and intimate observers alike; he looked different. It was not that he did not look human; of course, he did. But there was something else, something *off,* but not negative; something *more,* but not better; perhaps something further along the evolutionary trail. Facial features were slightly elongated, more than Asian-mixed people, more than those of full blood from the Orient or anywhere else. Looking into the eyes of this person, which were larger than average, was to feel that he could read your personal file in the Akashic Records and decipher every word. Your deepest secrets could find no closet in which to hide from his perceptive gaze. While warm-hearted in demeanor and action, Mikael's exceptional energy, coupled with youthful discontent, saturated his presence and sparked a concern for one-upmanship and impatience for those he thought were lesser than him. And he *did* think some folk were less than him, an immoral trait no matter how advanced the species that might have spawned him.

Human topics, practically all of which are laced with competitiveness, amplified his coarser characteristics. Yet, when discussing UFO contacts and alien interventions, calm filled his persona that backwashed the sharpness of his personality and drowned the rough edges with unusual maturity. While revealing his story, the normally non-emotional Mikael dropped a bucket of tears.

Basically, he was a twenty-something guy groping to discover who he was, no matter *who* he was. Only DNA testing might show if he is an alien hybrid, or not. But that would involve a painstaking long and expensive process, and one that Mikael could not afford and would not tolerate. And genetics, currently, is steeped in disease prevention studies; and *not concerned* about possible extraterrestrial manipulation of DNA in humanity. Even if it was, it would be years before the answers would be conclusive.

Yet, everyday, more and more people are telling their stories of abduction from all around the world. Saipan would be no different. Perhaps Mikael's mother was such a victim. It would be easy for aliens to fly into Saipan, grab someone, and fly out long before jets would be scrambled from Andersen Air Force base on Guam Island, about 140 miles southwest. That is, if the UFO was ever picked up on radar. The speed that UFOs can accomplish is well documented, so the approach to Saipan from, let's say, the North Pacific could be undetected. Skimming along a few feet above the water, under radar, would take a UFO about one second to reach the island.

While most of us are not comfortable with the idea that alien hybrids may live amongst non-hybrids, the ever-growing acceptance of the ancient alien theory that we are only here *because* of alien intervention and design may develop to be the reality. And would it be so unusual for a parenting species to improve the "plants" by engineered tinkering with their abilities to survive and perpetuate? Of course not, our scientists do it in laboratories around the world everyday – usually *without* the subject's permission.

Was Mikael's mother taken and impregnated with alien sperm to create a hybrid son? Could her fetus's DNA have been altered after a normal conception? Does it matter? While most humans would insist on some physical proof of his story, Mikael is not pressed to comply. Discussion of his encounters with aliens rarely happens. Enough side glances from people come due to his physical appearance alone. No point adding a glaze to their eyes by claiming visits from spacemen. Of the few people with whom he has mentioned his experiences, he simply does not care if they believe him or not. There is no proof.

I can attest to this attitude. *Evidence* of alien visits on our planet is either completely *absent*, or at best, *circumstantial*. Yet, under my left breast is a scoop mark received when I was visited in *my* bedroom at age thirteen by an alien gray. With a metal object, he scraped a piece of my skin away. It never bled and it never formed a scab and healed normally. It remains a small scoop mark. No, I do not know why they did that. Does the mark prove my story? No. In most people's minds, that mark is the result of a thousand different possibilities. And they are right. The scoop could easily have been from something else.

But it is not. It is only there because of gray alien tampering.

Mikael's reasoning is similar, in that he has the truth, but no physical evidence to prove it.

Mary says that Mikael is more comfortable with his memories now. His human and alien breeding propel him through society, grappling with earthly problems and solutions in a not altogether earthly way, perhaps. Life is no easier or harder for him than for anyone else.

Does he believe he is a hybrid? He's not sure. When he asks himself that question, his head screams "no," but his heart, the organ that never lies, whispers "yes."

To be part E.T. and part earthman leaves Mikael feeling out of *every* place. He strives for peace between his two halves and hopes only to be thought of as a good man.

He better be good. There are a lot of parents watching.

Chapter 14

HOME RUN
Sergeantsville, Hunterdon County

"Your present circumstances don't determine where you can go; they merely determine where you start."

—*Nido Qubein*
Author, businessman, consultant, and educator

A cigar-shaped object hung motionless in the sky.

It was July 1964 and the atmosphere was sunny and blue at 7:45 p.m. Eleven year-old Todd and his two cousins had just finished winning their Little League game against the Stockton, New Jersey, team and were heading home to Sergeantsville. His aunt piloted the '59 DeSoto Fireflite and chatted with her mother in the front seat. On the "mile-long" rear bench, Todd and his two cousins tussled.

They were heading northeast on Route 523 out of Stockton. About halfway along the route was a slight incline. As the car puttered upward, somebody called, "What is that?"

His aunt immediately saw the sight in question and pulled the vehicle off to the side of the road so that everyone could look at "it." Four occupants hopped out of the car; grandmother dragged herself out, and all moved around to the front of the auto, gazing up as they went. The two women huddled together near the chrome front bumper as an unspoken safeguard, but the three boys plowed off the road into the adjacent field. Enthusiastic faces looked upward, unsure of what to make of the strange air machine.

Todd was expecting loud engine sounds and quick maneuvers. He would be surprised.

Due east, on the *right* side of the car, up in the air, was a cigar-like craft! It was the size and shape of a pencil held at arms-length, tubular with rounded ends. The ship was dark gray in color, dull, not shiny, against the light-blue background of sky. It had a row of lights going down the side of it from left to right, and was thirty feet above the tree line, which was approximately sixty feet tall. The car idled 150 feet away from the vessel on the highway. It felt close. It *was* close. It was a UHO: unidentified hovering object. There was no movement; it edged neither left nor right, but stayed frozen as if held in place by an invisible hand. And there was no sound, a strange non-effect considering the device needed strong energy to fight gravity and remain still. Therefore, it was not an airplane, helicopter, or jet, since they are some of the noisiest inventions on the planet. Neither was it a balloon; it was long, thin, and without cords, strings, or any attachments. This thing was nothing that Todd or his family had ever observed before.

As if orchestrated by the gods to show a comparison, there was a single-engine airplane flying north of this UHO off the *left* side of the parked car, and the sound from the airplane was easily apparent. Being on the opposite side of the heavens, the sound could only have been from the plane.

The relatives watched the strange cylindrical craft for ten minutes. They wondered: who put it there, who was flying it, why didn't it move, and what was its purpose?

Finally, Todd's aunt decided it was time to go. For the rest of the ride home, everyone spoke at once. The cylinder was the most fascinating thing that any of them had ever seen. Back at Todd's house, all five people burst into the kitchen and related to Todd's mother what they could about the amazing event. The "party" then spread out onto the back deck, where sky-watching and UFO discussions captured adult interests. The kids held their own counsel, their imaginations soaring, their hopes for another sighting mounting by the instant. Everyone chattered about the strange flying craft, what it was, what it was *not*, and what it all meant.

A year later, in October 1965, Todd would watch a news report from New Hampshire on the Betty and Barney Hill abduction case, and it began to dawn on him that the idea of aliens visiting this world was reality.

Todd was, and still is, amazed by his experience. There was no fear. He had never heard much about alien spaceships up to that point, even though some of his friends were into sci-fi magazines and "B" movies. Todd himself had never involved his psyche in galactic travel. Baseball was his first love. But *after* the sighting, he began picking up books and magazines on UFOs. Todd wishes he knew then what he knows now. Books filled him with info on the greys, reptilians, mantises, and humanoids, as well as saucers, globes, triangles, boomerangs, and myriads of close encounters. That cigar-UFO would have been knocked out of the park with identifications and suppositions. At worst, it got him started on a lifelong venture to learn the truth about alien visitation.

When they drove away that night, the cigar-object was still hanging motionless in the sky. Todd wishes that the family had stayed longer to study it, had waited till it made a move, or had done something out of this world. If UFOs appeared *again,* Todd would stick with it till the end. He would pursue it around the countryside until he got an answer as to its origins and its intentions. And that info, he guessed, would be a new start to human existence.

Chapter 15

REVELATION
Lawrence Township, Mercer County

"In what way can a revelation be made but by miracles"

—William S. Paley
Co-founder, chief executive of
Columbia Broadcasting System (CBS)

Winston's first UFO experiences were at five years old in 1952 Lawrence Township. He would wait for his parents to go to bed and then filch his father's binoculars, slip out to the backyard, and lay on the grass to gaze upward. The UFOs truly *were*; he had no idea where the occasional dashing lights were from. Winston at five, and even later in life, never knew why he needed to look at the stars at such an early age, but it seemed of paramount importance. Starting also at that age, Winston had dreams of flying amongst those suns. He would sail through different galaxies. This near-nightly occurrence of the dream continued into his forties.

But was it purely a dream?

Knowing what is known now about the paranormal in various areas, namely out-of-body experiences, lucid dreams, and the ever-increasing numbers of people who recall their own alien abductions, the question screams: was it a dream?

In early June of 1954, at age seven, Winston and several of his cousins received their Holy Communion in the Catholic Church. His grandmother held a party at her farm in Lawrence Township to celebrate the important ritual. During the picnic, Winston's game-playing-running-around suddenly ceased as he glanced up. The sky was an ocean blue with a few island-clouds. It was not, however, the Peter Max-like heavens that stopped him.

What did stop him was a big, white, round object, visible three to four miles up in the air that was slightly north of the property. It sat motionless in the sky. The diameter of the sphere was close to the moon in size, solid in appearance; bright, but not from its own luminescence. And it certainly was *not* the moon because the moon was not visible that time of day.

Winston walked directly into an adjacent field and studied the strange object with a never-before-known delight. Something called to him without words, beckoned him without motion, appealed to his mind and emotions at the same time to be unafraid and look for and accept different things in the world. Even as a seven year old, he knew that this was something real *and* something from a far-off place. Someone had put it there and that someone would take it away. Winston was in love.

The rest of his family was now watching the strange ball of light.

So concerned was Winston's Uncle Jim about the object that he stopped partying, dashed into the house, and called the local newspaper to find out if they had any information about the flying phenomenon. The newspaper revealed that hundreds of people had already called wondering about the peculiar circle in the sky. Uncle Jim was also told that the newspaper had called McGuire Air Force Base near New Hanover Township, Burlington County, and requested information about the object. The Air Force scrambled several jets to hunt down the ball and intercept.

Winston, his family, and no doubt thousands of others got to witness the action. As the fighters approached the area, the communion party-goers were stunned when the rounded object simply vanished into thin air. That is, it did not fly away; it did not move away. It disappeared. After a few seconds, the Air Force jets flew by into empty air. The chase was over.

The party quickly turned from festivity to wonderment about the impossible appearance and disappearance of the unnatural ball. But without real answers to the bounteous questions, attention reverted back to sodas and sandwiches, beer and pretzels, and child-like games.

Winston remained in the field, waiting for a return performance from the device that he knew was nearby, just out of eye sight, but that did not come.

Princeton, Mercer County

In the summer 1980, Winston was thirty-three years old. He was motoring to work in Florham Park along Route 206, north of Princeton, pumping himself up for his position as executive vice-president of a bank. The weather was calm and the sky only partly clouded.

He was surprised to catch a glimpse of a metallic object through the upper left corner of his windshield. It was high in the air.

Suddenly from the object, a flash of lightning struck his vehicle. It was a perplexing flash in that it was not a "conventional" bolt of lightning, but more like a ball. Yet it was not "ball lightning," since that originated only in a storm atmosphere with high humidity. That day in 1980 was not stormy or humid. Also, the ball in the air appeared metallic. Ball lightning has never been reported to look like metal.

Upon pounding his car with energy, the entire inside of the auto glowed like a 1,000 watt bulb. This only lasted for a second, not even enough time to react. Plus, Winston's fifteen years of driving habits locked his attention on traffic.

That attention, amazingly, *was* torn away by a little finger.

The pinky finger of his left hand was touching metal at the time of the flash and it instantly went numb (it is numb to this day) and his whole hand was on pins and needles.

More than just a lightning strike, Winston suddenly became filled with something he could only describe as partial enlightenment. He suddenly had a new understanding of the Bible, which he had not looked at in decades. Concepts of the universe shrank and became manageable, something that he felt he could easily figure out. Business acumen increased tenfold and his work responsibilities now seemed childlike. Mysteries of health and wellbeing melted away and a belief in his own abilities to not only cure himself, but also heal others, blossomed. All of this filled his heart and spirit in an instant.

Despite his left hand tingling erratically (perhaps a plea for medical attention), a search for a church became his first necessity after recovering from the initial shock of the lightning strike. Lessons taught from the pulpit every Sunday had not prepared Winston for strange bolts from heaven, or for him to become the recipient of a modern miracle. He needed some answers and he needed them now.

Winston zipped to the nearest Catholic Church only a block off Route 206, parked, and dashed for the front door of the rectory. At that early hour, he was welcomed with a touch of reserve, but offered coffee as the reverend listened impatiently from behind an old oak desk in his office. The man shifted nervously in his chair, glancing out the window more than once as attention to Winston's details waxed and waned. When Winston finished his tale, the holy man leaned back and folded his arms across his crucifix.

"I think you're on drugs," he concluded.

Winston was insulted and returned the insults in kind with several four-letter words.

His Church had disappointed him. He plowed back into his car and continued his now agitated journey towards work in Florham Park.

On the way, he approached his favorite stop-over, the Somerville Flea Market in Somerville, the halfway point between home and work. He often took a five-minute respite there to unwind before starting his day of drudgery at the bank. Everything about him felt slightly different after the light-flash filled him and the inside of his car. Today's stop was necessary; a needed browse of the infinite wares of the vendors if only to ground-out the shock of a bolt of strange energy.

No sooner had he started perusing than a woman approached him and quickly asked, "Excuse me, sir, may I speak to you for a moment?" Winston took a half step back because of the woman's unusual high intensity. For a split second, he thought she would attack.

"Why certainly," he responded as politely as the moment would allow, his eyes darting around for co-conspirators, and moving his right hand to his wallet in an anti-pickpocket maneuver.

"I have to tell you, that you glow."

Winston was used to people sharing their "opinions." His realtor had shared that Winston needed to spend more money on a bigger house for more "prestige." Customers shared that loan rates at his bank were immorally too high. His neighbor shared that he needed to cut the lawn once a week instead of every two.

No one had ever shared before that he was radiant.

"What the heck does that mean?" Winston asked with as much amusement as confusion. "I don't understand."

"You are surrounded by an enormous amount of bright light. I am blessed with the ability to see people's auras, but I have never seen one as powerful as yours." The woman was carrying a large pocketbook and from its interior she extracted a brand-new Bible, which she handed to Winston accompanied by a warm smile. "Read this," she said, as she pressed the book into his unwilling hands. "You will find several stories here of interest. Most important, there will be tales of other people who carry such a powerful aura around them, people that you know."

With that, the woman turned and strolled away, disappearing in a few moments among the crowd of energetic shoppers. Winston would never see her again.

Upon arriving home that night, he placed the Bible in a drawer in his kitchen, thinking that someday he would get to reading it and search out the stories the woman alluded to. But he never did, feeling that his recent "upgrade" by the light qualified all he needed to know.

He had been zapped by an energy beam that filled him with "instant knowledge," then was accosted by a soothsayer at the flea market, telling him how shiny he was and giving him a free book. Maybe the aura she saw was an after-effect of the lightning strike; perhaps the strange plasma beam enhanced and enlarged his psychic being and spread it beyond his human body.

Perhaps it was nothing at all. Two points were clear: Winston knew his life was evolving in a para-terrific way; and his pinky was numb.

Weeks later, the bank insisted that all employees receive a physical examination as part of their health maintenance program. This gave Winston a chance to inquire about the problem with his left hand and learn more about his general health, something he was becoming increasingly aware of. At the doctor's office, he was instructed by a nurse to remove his clothing, hop on the table, and wait for the examining doctor.

Approximately ten minutes later, the nurse returned to the room to apologize for the delay. But when she looked at Winston sitting on the table she jumped back! At first he thought his lack of clothing had stunned the nurse in some way. Perhaps he had misunderstood; maybe he was not supposed to be naked, and now the woman's moral values had been put to the test.

Suddenly, she blurted out, "I can't talk to you now, but would you please see me after work, around 4:30? I have something urgent I want to discuss with you." To his own surprise, Winston immediately agreed to this meeting, though he was not sure why. Dating had always been done through conventional introductions from friends or by contact at a local watering hole. The recent paranormal developments he had experienced, however, had thrown a brick through the fragile glass windows of his life. Metal globes shooting bolts of light at his car, sudden information surges, and strangers accosting him about auras apparently would not be the end results. Now, a lovely nurse was asking him for a date while he sat naked in her office.

"Sure, I'll meet you at 4:30."

That afternoon, Winston and the nurse locked eyes in the doctor's parking lot. She touched him on the arm and looked deep into his heart. The forwardness startled him, suggesting a romantic tryst, if not a long-term relationship.

Then she asked, "Do you believe in life on other planets?" Whether it was the question he was hoping for or not was ambiguous, yet it was one he was happy to answer.

"Not only do I believe, but I *dream* about it almost every night." He referred to the flying dream that whisked him beyond the solar system.

"Well, your dreams are about to come true," she teased with a sincere smile.

Sandra, the nurse, then invited Winston to meet her at her friend June's house in Northeast Philadelphia. This was to take place a couple days later. The reason was unspecified beyond "you'll see."

Sounding less like a date and more like an Amway-pyramid-sales meeting, Winston was unsure. His head told him he was wasting his time. Why would this woman want him to meet her and a friend across the river in Northeast Philly unless it was to deal in drugs or buy Avon? But she implied that aliens would somehow be involved. How was that possible? While seemingly level-headed enough, Sandra and her Northeast Philly friend, June, might be two "Lizzie Bordens" in disguise, planning to steal his car and wallet and dice him into salad-size meat portions.

Then his heart kicked-in its Olympic swimming pool-sized opinion. Winston's recent partial enlightenment began to respond. Why would Sandra's first serious question to him be about aliens? There were at least seven or eight thousand other topics she could have broached. What made her think that such a question would have captivated his interest? Was she psychic? Intuitive? Or something else? Winston felt at a deep level that she was trustworthy. Despite his mind's caution about safety, its *number one concern*, his heart valves flapped happily over the prospect of spending time with the two ladies of alien mystery, knowing at sub-levels that something good might come of it.

Two days later, upon his arrival at the Northeast Philly apartment, June answered the door, looked at Winston, and said, "I have a message for you."

"From who?" he asked with reserve, feeling awkward in the hallway.

"From your space brothers."

Despite Winston's openness, this was all growing a bit strange, even for him. She escorted him into the living room where Sandra was sitting. After brief greetings, June retrieved a paper from the kitchen table, then joined the others in the living room. She proceeded to read from the paper a long letter, written in freehand.

The letter was a description of Winston, inside and out. It revealed deep aspects of who he was, including ultra-personal feelings he harbored about a number of things that were kept secret from the world. This letter, whose author he was dying to have revealed, fit him to a tee and made his nerve endings understandably scratchy. Upon hearing the final words, he broke into tears. It was literally a better self-portrait than he himself could have described.

June gave him the note.

Winston studied the letter in the vague hope he would recognize the perpetrator's penmanship. Wording was elegant, more beautiful than any of his family, friends, or acquaintances could pen. Grammar was richer than Shakespeare, smoother than Fitzgerald. The words were so amazingly perfect that he knew June, who came across smarter on a street than in a book, could not possibly have made them up on her own. Even Sandra, who displayed a bit more refinement than her friend, still lacked the savvy to double-life herself as a woman of letters. In fact, neither woman could have created one word of the letter, since they did not know Winston from a Tastykake cupcake, and research and background checks would have brought only the most basic personal information in that pre-Internet time. Couple these facts with Winston's own assuredness that the staggeringly personal nuances of his inner-most beliefs had *never* been put on parade for anyone. In short, the CIA and KGB combined could not have compiled such details of his personality in two days.

"Where did you get this?" Winston now demanded.

"I wrote it," was June's simple answer.

"No you didn't." Winston grabbed a nearby paper from another table and desperately shoved it in front of the calm June.

"Write something. And don't try to disguise your handwriting." June picked up a ballpoint and wrote a short sentence. She wrote freely, with confidence, as if she were writing a quick hello to an old friend. Winston snatched the paper as she finished, though he could already see the writing style was nothing like the original letter. He waved the new note in June's face.

"This doesn't match."

"That's because the original was done in automatic writing. Do you know what that is?"

June's attitude was sure, almost smug. These women had answers for everything, Winston thought.

"I've heard of it, but…"

"It means the spirit, or perhaps in this case, the energy of someone else works through me to write out on a piece of paper the information it wants us to have. Pretty cool, huh?"

Winston was silent for a moment. His mind kicked a few facts to the forefront. One: no one knew this much personal information about him. Two: even if he had slipped up in the past and shared a piece or two of personal data with *someone,* there was *no way* these two wacky women would have been able to track down these facts and present them in a penned letter that was futuristic in its uncanniness and renaissance in its artistic form.

Still, the note had elicited deep feelings from Winston, something that even intimate partners who had known him for years would have been hard-pressed to accomplish. Odder still was that the letter released a truer part of himself to the surface. He had grown with its reading and become a bigger person than the one who had walked into the small unkempt apartment in Philadelphia only minutes earlier. It was something he was glad for, hoped for, and it edged him closer to his lifelong dream, something that Sandra hinted about days before in the doctor's parking lot.

"Sandra, is it really true that someone from another planet, some faraway place wants to contact me?"

And as he stared through damp eyes, deep into Sandra's, Winston's world began to shake.

Sandra's eyes suddenly grew to three times the normal human size. They resembled eyes from a wild Bengal tiger, but still soft with kindness, and emanating a mastery of some distant knowledge. Their color washed from a dull blue to a neon-green!

Winston's body jerked away. He was at once repelled and allured. He was about to ask what the hell was going on when she suddenly said:

"If you could see *your* eyes right now, Winston, you would understand."

His jaw fell about two feet below his chest as his flabbergasted mind tried to grasp onto a concept with no handles. Did he hear it right? Was this woman with the weird/sexy eyes saying that he too now had eyes the size of golf balls that resembled some giant alien cat? Sandra's unusual optics continued to gaze into him like a sci-fi character from a 3-D movie screen.

His hands flew to his face. Something felt wrong.

Winston jumped from his plush chair and began running around the apartment looking for a mirror. By the time he hit the bathroom, his panting, heaving body saw only a familiar reflection in the glass. His eyes were normal as every day. He marched back to Sandra and clumped next to her.

Sandra's eyes were human again.

"My eyes have not changed," Winston moaned a bit with disappointment, slightly unsure, but marveled by the return of Sandra's eyes to a standard female appearance. Grabbing his head in his hands, trying to rub away the ache of absorbing too much information too fast, unsure of who he was and where he was, Winston wished for normality and hoped that answers would come in the next couple of sentences.

"They *did* change," Sandra assured him. "But now they are normal again, just like mine. You would never be able to maintain those eyes for very long."

"I don't suppose you could explain that."

"Never. It's not for me to explain." The cryptic answer irritated Winston worse than the messages in the 1950s sci-fi "B" movies: "Keep watching the skies." Yeah, whatever.

Nobody had ever talked to him like this before. His world of debits and credits, of investments and defaults, was spiraling away through his fingers, leaving him with the temptation to learn who he really was – that in an existence of historic repetition, of economic slavery, and trite technical improvements, he was by every account...a person of interest.

"What am I to do now? I don't know what to do; you have to help me." A strange thing happened with this request. Winston sensed a different part of himself, a larger part, a higher-self powering the request. It was softer, more trusting than he would normally be under the condition of having met one of these women only twice and the other only once. His heart felt strong, awash with agape, and as big as Ocean County, New Jersey.

"Okay," Sandra said, "let's have some fun."

The trio walked down to a neighborhood park only about three blocks from the apartment. The women armed Winston with a 35mm camera to carry on his chest, strapped about his neck. The plan was for him to walk around the park and, without thinking, and whenever he felt the urge, to snap the shutter button with the camera aimed at the sky. Despite the recent miracles in the apartment, Winston kept his trigger finger locked on skepticism.

"What is that going to do?" he said, his voice sounding almost like a complaint.

"We'll find out." Sandra and June had slight smirks on their faces as they turned and left Winston on his own.

Over the next hour, Winston pointed the lens at the sky and, on occasion, snapped a picture. Confusion was his only company and plagued him with questions about why he was doing this. As far as he could see, there was nothing in the sky but the usual stars – not an overly exciting exhibit .

The next day, he took the film to his local pharmacy to have it developed. A couple days later, he retrieved the finished prints.

To his amazement every other photo contained an object streaking across the sky, none of which had he seen with his naked eye during the night of photography. What did this mean?

The two unusual women had also instructed Winston to visit his local park by himself. He was to look for alien globes, the basketball-size illuminated spheres that tended to hang out in parks, cities, rural and forested areas. This he did, but was unable to find even a single UFO. However, when he headed for home, a strange bright white light – basketball size – appeared out the left side of his front windshield at an indeterminable distance. No matter which direction he turned, the light stayed in the exact same position in his windshield throughout the journey home, keeping pace with his heading and speed. Though often blocked by trees or buildings, the strange globe would be visible again in the next clearing. This lasted for almost an hour. But when he neared his street, the globe was gone.

As the ensuing weeks slipped by, Winston received daily calls from Sandra. He was fond of her as a person, but as a romantic interest, he considered her not his type.

"Look, Sandra, if I'm going to take part in this alien business or project or whatever you call it, I'm going to need your help. And in this case that means I don't want you around. While I think you're a great person, there's something about you that gives me the willies. I seem to vibrate in some very uncomfortable fashion anytime that you are near and I just want to run away. So could you *please* respect this request and stop calling. Let's allow the program to progress on its own and I'll keep you posted whenever I feel that it's necessary."

"But I want to make a baby with you," Sandra cooed over the phone as if it was the most natural thing in the world to say to a man she'd only known for less than a month.

"I don't feel like I could do that with you," Winston's words winched out of his mouth, hardly believing his own statement that was sending away a beautiful woman with whom he could have had sex if he chose. Heart and mind, however, for one of the few times in their coexistence within him, were actually on the same page. From that point on, Sandra behaved. Sort of.

Though the phone harassment stopped, Winston did on occasion continue to consort with the two ladies.

On one occasion at his local park, they told him to watch the skies because in ten minutes a bright light, "the ship," was going to appear. Exactly ten minutes later that was what happened. A large light, bigger than any star yet smaller than a full moon, popped into the sky and hung there for almost a full minute before vanishing in the same fashion.

Jackson Township, Ocean County

While the miracles brought on by Sandra and June seemed to compound as time went on, Winston's human nature started to rail, thinking that all he had seen may have somehow been pre-designed to fool him. The Moony movement was in full bloom at that time and Winston had suspicions that perhaps Sandra and June were leading him into a gigantic scam. He felt he needed help.

He contacted his friend Marge, a paranormal aficionado and ghost-hunting specialist, and filled her in on the goings-on of the Sandra/June team and the preponderance of marvels that they had evoked.

"Marge, would you please go out with me tonight and search for UFOs?" He felt a need for corroboration to any further fantastic events.

"Sure, I'd be glad to." She seemed as excited about the content of the plan as she did about accompanying her good friend.

Off Exit 16 of Interstate I-195, left on Anderson Road, left onto Perrineville Road, right onto Reed Road for about a half mile, then right onto a dirt road in Jackson Township, behind Six Flags Great Adventure they sped. Winston pulled his car into a desolate spot, where he and Marge armed themselves with flashlights, cameras, and binoculars. The hours ticked by.

Nothing happened.

"Here I am," Winston called out inside the car bouncing the words around the headliner and leather upholstery. "Show me something impressive. I brought a friend with me, so put on a show that we both can witness." But the skies were quiet; the wooded surroundings empty of alien interest.

After two hours of doing nothing, Winston said, "This is boring, Marge, we might as well go."

"I'm with you, Winston."

"Give me a minute to run over to those bushes and take a break, and then we'll get out of here and get something to eat," Winston called as he hurried to the shrubs for a station break, slamming the car door behind him.

When his business was finished, he noticed a neon green light off in the distance. It was the same color green as Sandra's eyes had been weeks before. It was round and it began growing. Closer, at a cautious steady pace, it flew towards him. At about thirty-feet away, it came to a halt. Then it quickly bloomed into a large oblong, approximately three-and-a-half feet wide by two feet tall. The object then drifted towards the ground and disappeared into the earth, leaving behind the human embodiment of Sandra.

While Winston was thoroughly mesmerized by the magic of the green ball, its oblong-morphed condition, and the three-ring circus act of bringing Sandra's person to this desolate field in central New Jersey, all in ways beyond scientific explanation, his deep set morality was still able to find a voice in the face of the impossible.

"Sandra, you promised to leave me alone during these alien encounters." He tried to sound as pleasant as he could while still maintaining a shred of authority; make no mention that his knees were quivering like those of a three-year-old packed in ice.

Sandra smiled.

"Okay," she said. With that one word, her body popped like a bubble gum balloon and vanished in half a second.

Winston returned to the car and explained to Marge, with all the sincerity and level-headedness he could muster, exactly what she had missed. The look on her face could have sunk a thousand ships. But a quick change from her brought a soft grin and sympathetic eyes. Marge was concerned for her friend and decided he needed an immediate distraction.

Night shot of area where Sandra mysteriously appeared.

"Tomorrow night, let me take you on a ghost investigation. A woman says her house is haunted."

"Why would she think that?" Winston wondered, still shaking, longing for coffee, backing the car around and gassing it towards the nearest diner.

"Well, for one thing, when she puts a freshly baked apple pie on the living room mantelpiece to cool and walks away from it, it ends up on the dining room table."

"Ghosts would be a nice relief right about now. I'm getting a little tired of alien drama."

But he was not that tired of it. A test of his sanity was in order. Once he was home, he shot for the phone and called Sandra.

"Sandra, where were you at 8:30 tonight?" Winston politely demanded. "It's important that you tell me."

After a two-second pause, Sandra replied, "You know *damn well* where I was at 8:30. I was watching you pull up your zipper."

Winston was floored.

"You promised to leave me alone," he scolded like a father-figure.

"Sorry," she replied, less sorry, more amused.

"Maybe a time will come for us," Winston offered reservedly, "but not now."

"Okay," the woman with alien tendencies said with an upswing of hope on the end of the word. Winston bid a cautious good-bye.

Fraud played no part in that night's miracle, Winston knew. No one could have manufactured what he saw. And he had not asked Sandra to identify *his* actions at that time. He had only asked what *she* was doing. Her volunteering the minor fact that he had relieved himself in the brush was detail specific, too accurate for a guess. While some claim could be made that psychic ability brought her the information before or as Winston was calling her, so that the ready answer would suggest she *was* there when she was not, *no psychic ability* would have produced the green oblong that transmogrified into her physical presence in such a remote empty area while Winston and Marge happened to be there.

He then called June, Sandra's cohort in alien communications, and explained to her what had happened that night. But no sooner had he relayed the odd facts surrounding his evening, than June detonated her own bombshell.

"I have another message for you."

"You gotta be kidding?"

"Another message from your space brothers."

"Now what?"

"It reads: 'we do not make ourselves available upon your demands.'" The words came haltingly as if seen for the first time. The phone line got empty-quiet and frosty cold. Winston knew there was nothing else to say. He made his good-byes and hung-up.

From that time on, Winston often visited that remote area behind Six Flags in central Jersey. The trips were unaccompanied; he wanted the time for himself and any experiences to be his own without dragging friends, family, or the curious into an area of such great unknowns. On some four out of ten occasions, he witnessed UFOs crossing the heavens. They were each red in color, at least two miles up, and they zipped from horizon to horizon in no more than seven seconds. He was sure they were not meteors due to their matching appearances, and their level trajectories across the sky, not downward towards destruction. Nor were the red objects satellites since their arrival did not correlate with published timetables.

Winston would later tell comrades about his adventures and despite his initial wish to keep the sightings personal, the excited badgering of his friends to take them along with him overcame his need for aloneness.

Much like an amusement guide, Winston would take a friend or two at a time to the designated spot and more often than otherwise the corroborator saw a UFO. It was always a globe or a distant light, moving irrationally, sucking *ohs* and *ahs* from the private audience.

Hamilton Township, Mercer County

A couple of years passed and Winston was craving more.

Driving south on the New Jersey Turnpike one late summer night, he witnessed a bright light flying up in the sky. It was off the left side of his windshield like the globe he had seen years before in his local park.

He knew what it was, so he spoke to it.

"Please, I've been 100 percent sincere with you. But if you really are somebody who wants to see me, would you please show me some sign? Please give me something to hold onto."

Suddenly, the light began revolving in circles; it spiraled up and down, it dashed off to become a dot in the atmosphere, then flew down at incredible speed, stopping just yards above the ground, revealing itself to be close to a dozen feet across. It continued to gyrate for several minutes.

Winston's UFO elation quickly deteriorated his seventy mph driving skills.

He flew off the Turnpike at exit 7A, took I-195 west to Exit 5A, keeping the bouncing light in view. No longer clear if he was following it or vice versa, he was sure that he *did not* want to take it home. The car raced south on Route 130 a couple blocks to Klockner Road. He skidded left on Klockner, then a final jerk left on a dirt road into what at the time was a huge cornfield (it is in 2014 CE a Walmart department store). He slammed his car down the dirt path several hundred feet away from Klockner Road, so that it would not be visible to traffic. With a gravelly, dust-filled stop, he turned off the engine, hopped out of the vehicle, and kept his eyes on the flying light, which was only a few dozen yards away and had, essentially, led him to this spot.

All at once, a sensation filled Winston's head. It felt like two quick clicks of a stiff light switch.

The next thing he knew he was standing outside a magnificent flying saucer. It was a brushed steel-gray color, flat on the edge with numerous windows, seamless in every direction and about 200 feet in diameter. Whether he was still in the cornfield or not, he was not certain, but there were a few absolutes. This saucer was beautiful, it was "wow." It was a fulfillment of Winston's life-longing to be part of the fuller Universe, or Universes, that he knew – deep in his being – existed beyond Earth's childlike three-dimensional nursery.

Overcome with joy, relieved from doubt, Winston did find one serious problem and he began to laugh. An unknown voice immediately manifested inside his mind and asked, "Why are you laughing?"

"Because I've waited my whole freakin' life to see you and I can't find the door to get in!" The inner voice responded, "You don't need a door. Simply be with us."

The next thing he knew he was standing inside the spacecraft. He was in a white room about twenty feet wide, about ten feet deep. "They" had him sit on a table.

"They" were humanoid, similar body structure to earthlings, shorter, but with bald heads, and even with skin-tight suits their sexuality was indeterminate. Skin color had a bluish tint and ears were smaller. The eyes were larger in proportion to their heads (similar to Sandra's temporary ocular display), with cat-like irises grayish in tone. Since "they" were moving in and out of the room, Winston's best guess was that there were about nine of them.

There was one other great distinction about the visitors: they were not solid. At one point during his visit, Winston saw two of them *pass right through each other* as they walked about the room. Was it all a hologram sent from another planet, galaxy, universe, dimension, reality? He did not know, nor did he have the ability to ask the question, since it was only one among millions pounding at his brain fighting to get out.

It is at this point that most abductees feel terror or confusion at being "a captive" of a foreign species. But Winston had a different feeling. He felt like he had been invited by family. A sense of being home was stronger here than with any place he had ever lived on earth in his entire life. The camaraderie must have been mutual because the aliens did something they are not famous for doing: they asked his *permission to do an examination.*

"Sure, be my guest," was his radical, trusting reply. A thorough physical was performed without pain, without discomfort, and in a short period of time. This included rectal, naval, eyes, ears, nose, and throat inspections. Still, Winston felt more comfortable in the hands of their examiner than he did in the hands of any human doctor. Could that have been due to it somehow being a remote energy-base exam as opposed to truly physical? No answer was or is available.

Then a stranger thing happened. The alien asked Winston to tell him about his life. So he did.

Another surprise question was: do you have any friends? And of course Winston answered that he did. But, he told them, one thing that always pestered him during his life was that he was never able to find anyone who he felt truly comfortable with, somebody who was just like him, one who saw the world as a bigger place, as part of an infinite-eternal space. He also noted that he believed his feelings ran deeper than others, and because of their depth, he never felt comfortable sharing his sentiments because he never felt appreciated. On the rare occasion when he did let loose rich mawkishness, he was pushed away by listeners, perhaps because he was overbearing, perhaps because they were unable to understand, perhaps both.

The alien gave an unexpected answer to this. "That is because you are not from here."

"Then where am I from?"

"Would you like to see?"

"More than anything."

First, they gave Winston a tour of the ship, showed him its ins and outs, ups and downs, though he could not understand a fraction of what they were talking about. When he asked what powered the craft, they simply replied "consciousness." He tried to follow up with questions to learn more about that, but was told that it was too complex for him at that time.

Right in the middle of the ship, on the floor, were three items. They appeared to be crystals. But they were so big that Winston doubted they were actually crystals like those found on Earth. He was told that depending on how the crystals were turned, that was the direction in which the ship flew.

After this brief, if confusing, tour of the vessel, Winston was told that they were going to be on their way.

Within a couple moments, Winston was shown a screen that revealed the ship was now hovering about 100 feet off the ground of an entirely different planet.

His first thought was: *could this be real?*

Observations told him that this was an Earth-like place. There was greenery; there was a bluish sky; there seemed to be air, or at least atmosphere of some makeup. The giveaway that it was not Earth was the leaves. The leaves on the trees and bushes were "different," accumulatively giving the whole scene a jagged texture versus the softness of Earth greenery.

And miraculously, there was a young boy walking along a wooded area below the ship.

"Do you see the boy?" Winston was asked and he affirmed that he did. "That was you when you lived on our planet."

"But I was born in New Jersey; I had a mother and a father."

"Yes, you were, and yes, you did, but before that, you were here."

Next, he was shown a city made of glass, built into the side of a mountain, but the reason for seeing it was unclear.

And then it was over.

In the next instant, Winston was standing next to his car back on planet Earth. The saucer was gone. If there were cordial good-byes, he did not remember.

Surrounding corn swayed in a scratchy cacophony as late summer breezes swiped across. The night was complete with the usual insect sounds and a dark starry heaven.

Winston felt whole. The biggest wonderings of who he was and where he was from had finally replaced their question marks with periods, and the revelations had come in a style most spectacular.

He happily burst into laughter again, not from the delight in discovering the answers to some of life's great mysteries, but because he still had to drive home.

And to do that, he had to open the car door.

Chapter 16

RED REVOLVER
Washington Twp., Mercer County

"It is indeed a desirable thing to be well-descended, but the glory belongs to our ancestors."

—Plutarch
Greek historian, biographer, and essayist

By Tuesday night, November 16, 1982, Lujza had lived in the United States about twenty-five years. Her American husband owned a construction company and had built her a beautiful hillside rancher with a swimming pool on Windswept Drive in Washington Township, Mercer County, about four miles southwest of Budd Lake. This existence was a polarization from her childhood in Isaszeg, Hungary, during World War II. The "old-country" went from pre-war pro-Axis fascism, to Nazi occupation, to bombardment by Soviet-Romanian forces in 1944-45. Her dream of a happy childhood had been perverted into everyday nightmares. After the war, her family felt North America would be a happier place.

Naturally, they moved to New Jersey.

That Tuesday she had been at the university where she studied art and photography. While the courses were tough or tedious, depending on which fellow student was asked, for Lujza the information came easy, since it was her passion. Red was her favorite color, and her current classroom project was a modernist version of an old Wild West .45 caliber pistol, done in acrylic, with the main color of the piece a threatening blood-red.

Home by seven o'clock, dinner done, textbooks resting on the kitchen table before the onslaught of homework, Lujza only then realized the odd empty feeling in the house. Not even her two dogs, Blackie and Pal, were around. Perhaps they had run away again. The stillness was palpable and crawled on her back like an ice iguana.

It was 8 p.m. She was sitting at the kitchen table with a cup of Maxwell House, but it did not warm her. Something about the night felt gloomier than the deepest Columbian dark roast at room temperature. Uneasiness kept her crossed right leg bouncing against her will under the table.

Suddenly, the house shook like a surprised infant.

Perhaps it was another gas explosion, like a previous one that occurred at a nearby company several years earlier. This was a "strange" shake, however. It was neither like the gas blow-up, nor anything close to the many explosions that ripped around her as a child in World War II Hungary.

She rose from the table with the intention of dashing through the dark dining room to the sliding glass doors that opened onto a large redwood deck.

She was close to the doors when a loud voice popped into her head. "Do not go out there. It is dangerous."

"Okay," she thought, "I'll stop at the sliding doors." There, she had a masterful view of the darkened valley. But immediately she noticed that the entire area was in a blackout. The normal dots of housing and streetlights were off. The lowlands were not simply obscure, they were invisible.

Then Lujza was startled by a blast of red radiance from above. Six large red lights were flying slowly over her house. They had materialized as if from a magic spell and were headed towards the neighbor's place on her left. Each light was round, about eighteen inches in diameter, and revolved in unison around a central point as if on a carousel, all the while moving northeast. Apparently, the lights were part of a larger device, but the darkness of the sky, of the area right behind the red lights, and the lack of local lighting made it impossible to see if in fact it was a ship. They could also have been tethered together somehow. Knowing for sure was impossible. The intensity of the blinding red lights only added to the problem since they were no more than thirty feet above her head. Lujza cracked the sliding door to the left to get a view unfiltered by glass and to listen for noise. Not only were the flying lights soundless, the entire outdoors seemed packed in a vacuum.

Lujza looked around in her wonderment, contemplating her next action. She gazed back to the kitchen to see that the entire house was dark. Had she turned off the lights? Was her house in a blackout like the rest of the valley?

Against better judgment, she slid the patio door left and walked out onto the deck. The noiseless rotating red lights were obviously not in a hurry, and continued to drift past her neighbor's house, which was also without lights, towards Budd Lake and beyond, vanishing over the heavy woods on the far side of the water.

Only five minutes had passed.

When she returned to the darkened kitchen, she switched on the lights, but they would not respond.

"What the heck is wrong with this?" Lujza wondered aloud. A few more flicks and fluorescence finally bathed the kitchen in cool white.

Lujza ran back to the patio door. The lights in the valley had all returned.

It is not provable that the electric failures in the area were due to the red lights, but it is most likely, since it matches stories from others who have experienced similar power outages during the presence of UFOs.

Lujza felt as if temporary insanity just signed a one-year lease.

But recovery was fast as she dumped several tons of red light information on her husband when he walked in the door. He was unsupportive, sadly, and any hopes of her revisiting the subject with him died with the break of dawn.

As with so many witnesses, Lujza began to look at life differently in the aftermath of this event. For her, it is plain that some of the beings visiting us, from wherever their origins might be, are the descendants of (or perhaps actually) our ancestors. They stop here to observe, to motivate, and to test us, weighing our worthiness to enter the grander Universal society. Certainly, Lujza knows that all aliens cannot fit under that umbrella of generalizing. It is clear in her mind that the species of ET that are the predecessors/engineers of our make-up could, and would, see us through difficulties not only like massive destructiveness (earthquakes, eruptions, floods, etc.), but also from intervention by dark-minded aliens bent on ill-will towards us.[1]

As if to highlight her new direction of thought, a purposeful incident occurred just after the red lights sighting.

At her high school graduation back in Isaszeg in the 1950s, a little black book made the rounds amongst the students. It was a black market science pamphlet that spoke about human origins coming from the stars rather than apes – about black holes, wormholes, space travel, and other fringe sciences. Lujza believed these were fairy tales for little girls, not for a young woman entering the real world. Somehow, within weeks after seeing the red globes, a copy of the little leaflet found its way back into her hands. Many of its far-out chapters, which in her youth appeared lunatic, now had plenty of mainstream proponents. And she was one of them.

Her understanding had turned around 360°, like the red globes that flew overhead.

Endnote

[1]There seems to be little evidence for "bad aliens." Note the general upbeat feel of each of the full-length stories in this book. Also see: *UFOS Above PA* and *Mid-Atlantic UFOs: High Traffic Area*, where numerous witnesses almost universally agree that, no matter how difficult the experience was to go through, it ended by being of the utmost importance to them over their lifetime. Most witnesses claim that they would never trade the experience, and the greater awareness that came with it, for anything in the world. I count myself in this group.

Chapter 17

SILVERY LINING INCLUDED?

East Windsor, Mercer County

"There are no rules of architecture for a castle in the clouds."

—Gilbert K. Chesterton
English writer and journalist

It could have been tedious for Benny that Sunday in May 1996. A repeat of hundreds of previous Saturdays and Sundays on second shift, guarding one of the buildings of the Carter-Walsh Pharmaceutical Company – the inventors of Arrid Extra Dry deodorant – was what he had expected.

That is not what he got.

The part-time security guard job near Old Trenton Road and Route 571 (Princeton-Hightstown Road) was a direct turnaround from his weekly work: a Ranger in a state park. As such, he answered park visitor's directional quandaries, relocated troublesome animals, and studied cloud formations for changing weather conditions, among other chores.

One security guard was assigned to each building on the Carter property, so Benny worked each weekend by himself. He spent half of his time in the tiny security office doing the minimal paperwork or reading the latest crime novel. Every half hour he did a walking key-tour to check that all doors were locked and that the building was secure. Weekend second-shift was extra quiet.

In both his jobs and his home life, Benny was easy-going, not easily shaken, and solved issues with the easiest solutions. Flights of off-beat imagination he did not permit himself, preferring the simple calm of a park glen or the solitude of an empty factory. His enforcement training had filed his eyes sharp for observation, so he instantly recognized the out-of-place, making him good at his jobs.

That Sunday around 5 p.m., he took a break from his novel and happened to look out the office window. He had an unhindered view of the sky and parking lot, looking east toward Cranberry Township. The upper air was packed with clouds, and a few of the formations were ominous.

One particular cloud, however, suddenly riveted his attention.

First, it was smooth, not wispy, straight, and long, supersized compared to all the other observable clouds, which resembled puffy bumping cars smashed together randomly across the heavens. Second, it was the darkest rain cloud that he had ever seen; and third, it hung well below all other clouds, perhaps by 500-1000 feet. The actual length of the cloud was indeterminate, but he guessed that it was well over a quarter of a mile long. It was moving northwest to southeast. It held his attention because it was different, darker gray, and it had an odd shape — cylindrical, not a profile that a cloud dashed about by a spinning planet stirring haphazard winds could long maintain.[1]

Further, against all reason, it seemed propelled.

At the "front" of the cloud, there was a swirling motion that extended a tad higher and lower than the main cloud body. Vaguely, it resembled a spinning vortex. This gyrating part of the cloud looked like it was pulling the entire formation forward faster than neighboring clouds above. And while the speed variation might be explained by perspective,[2] Benny felt the object was under its own power and intelligently operated.

He rose from his desk and dream-walked to the door for a clearer view, for though he trusted his sensory keenness, he could not justify in his head that a cloud could behave with a bizarre independence.

He continued to watch the thing for five minutes until it blended out of sight somewhere over Cranberry Township.

Though not given to fantasy, he was instantly haunted by the idea that there was something within the cloud, being cloaked, and moving through our skies for whatever purpose it had in mind. While of course he could not prove that either to himself or anyone else on Earth, the feeling would not leave him and would never leave him over the years of contemplation about the event.

Then a new idea struck.

Across the street from the Carter plant was a General Electric manufacturing facility. Part of their production at the GE plant was constructing components for NASA's many space programs. It dawned on Benny that the haunted feelings he had about the strange cloud was whether or not it could have been something created by GE for

NASA's use – or – with the plant involved in sensitive NASA programs, could the odd cloud and its clandestine operators be there to observe GE?[3]

As a state park ranger, most of Benny's weeks were spent out-of-doors. He had seen thousands of cloud formations over the decades, but not one of them ever gave him an ill feeling. The cylinder cloud provoked a sense of apprehension unlike anything the ranger/security man had ever felt before.

The weird cloud implied an act of construction rather than evaporation to Benny. Its impact on his memory was deep enough to become a permanent reason to take hard looks at clouds ever after. His nervous system that day screamed that there was much more to the cloud than met even the sharpest eyes. He just could not prove it.

Endnotes

[1] Truly cylindrical clouds do occasionally form naturally in the sky. In Australia, each fall, near the town of Burketown, Queensland, a tiny town of 200 or less residents, enormous tubular clouds form in a row of three or four cylinders. They are labeled "Morning Glory" clouds. Individual tubes can run for up to 600 miles long. They can also travel at up to 35 miles per hour, sometimes wreaking havoc with local aircraft. Nobody can explain the cause of this anomaly. Similar rounded-shaped clouds called "roll clouds" appear in various places around the globe, but are uncommon in New Jersey. These often occur during a collision of hot and cold fronts. The clouds resemble a large curved wall. In no way do they resemble the cylinder cloud described in the noted story.

[2] Two objects are moving at the same speed. One is close to you, the other is further away. The closer object will always appear to be moving faster.

[3] There's nothing new about UFOs buzzing around military/space installations or manufacturing plants involved with those industries. See: UFOs reported near Malmstrom Air Force Base, Fergus County, Montana on September 19, 2012 @ 10:19 p.m.

Also, I witnessed two alien globes floating in the desert near Edwards AFB in southern California in 2003. Such examples are numerous in UFO history.

Chapter 18

EASY CATCH
Ewing Township, Mercer County

"...behold, a stormy wind came out of the north, and a great cloud, with brightness around it, and fire flashing forth continually, and in the midst of the fire, as it were gleaming metal."

—*Ezekiel 1:1-28*
Holy Bible

Not that Luke cared, but it was May 10, 2008. He didn't care because it was the start of a promising two days off. It was Saturday. This was to be an easy weekend: no work, no UFO research. He had stopped to pick up his buddy, Mark, from his single home on Todd Ridge Road in Ewing Township. His friend was packing rods and clothes in preparation for two days of stellar quiet at Luke's summer house near Penn State in Central Pennsylvania. The plan was basic: perfect their fly fishing and pig-out on trout for dinner.

While his friend finished collecting his gear, Luke was standing on the side deck, looking across the Trenton-Mercer Airport, southeast. It was a bluebird day with a beckoning sky. Taking a break from work was a delight and as simple as a finger snap. Not quite so easy dumping UFOs out of his memory banks. That passion began when he was twelve, a result of several personal sightings.

A cigarette was pinched between the index and middle fingers of his right hand as he cozied-up to the handrail, resting on forearms, permitting the wood to take his weight. The tip of the butt grew bright as a long inhale soothed his body, but after half an exhale, the rest of the cloudy particles got snagged in his lungs as his body froze from a strange sight. His eyes blinked three times to assure him they were not lying.

Two huge lenticular craft, each surrounded by an orange haze, appeared in the near distance. They were only a couple hundred feet off the ground at a little less than two miles away, approximately over the Ewing Church Cemetery. Luke shot his left thumb horizontally up at full arms-length and was able to cover both ships, which would make them a considerable size at that short distance. The best guesstimate was they were about 150 feet across. He pulled his arm back and checked his watch: 7:02 a.m. There was no visual definition to them. Each was a smooth, solid piece of dull metal, flat on the bottom with a softly curving upper section, much like a glass lens. There were no lights, markings, wings, fins, or any protrusions whatever. On par with most UFO manifestations was the complete silence. As an avid UFO watcher, Luke's main tool was his camera. But since the next two days had been planned as a "vaca" weekend, he, regrettably, had left his beloved Nikon at home.

The vessels cruised across the sky swiftly and went out of sight in the northwest blue. For approximately ten seconds, Luke witnessed not one, but two images of an anomaly that an ever-shrinking majority of the human population insists do not exist.

And it was so easy. Anyone looking out their windows or standing on their property facing the cemetery that morning would have seen them. Why are scientists huddled in their laboratories or teacher's lounges when they should be up at seven o'clock in the morning searching the weekend skies with bare eyes? Some people argued with Luke that he was special, that "they" only appeared to him. That was unlikely.[1] Luke never felt or considered himself above or below anyone else. One simply needed to pay attention and look up often.

The twin alien craft's casual sailing through the air that morning, below-radar, struck him as being operated by pilots in no particular rush. And what were those pilots like? Why did they not land in the large yard below his friend's deck. There was enough room for at least one of the ships. All parties would have met; exchanged business cards. Luke would have invited them in to his friend's house for coffee and a cigarette, if they liked (Mark wouldn't mind), or better, the visitors would have taken Luke and his buddy for a ride to...everywhere.

A few moments later, his friend strolled out on the deck, decked out in his fisherman's wardrobe with a permit pinned to a camouflaged bucket hat.

"You're not going to believe me when I tell you this," Luke ruminated with inner laughter, wondering why anyone would believe him.

"Take your best shot." Mark looked quickly about the land and air, checking for oddities, knowing well his friend's proclivities.

"They're with us. I just saw too huge UFOs flying over the Ewing Church Cemetery."

"No way!"

"I wished you'd seen them."

"Well, yeah, I wished I'd seen them, too.

"I also wish I had my camera," Luke smashed his cigarette into the aluminum ashtray on the handrail.

"What did they look like?" Mark wondered. The story quickly retold, and Mark accepted Luke's experience unquestioned, since he knew well of his friend's multiple sightings over many years.

"They were gorgeous," Luke concluded.

"I've been meaning to tell you something," Mark said. "There have been three orbs hanging out over the cemetery every night. I wasn't sure if my eyes were playing tricks or what. But then my boss, who lives a couple streets over, asked me the other day: did I see those orbs that have been flying over the area lately?"

"You're kidding," Luke noted with mild surprise that so many people were making connections about UFO phenomena. It was a sign of the times.

Luke's interest in UFOs launched when he was twelve. He has made it to his fifties. Studies have brought him to the conclusion that there is not just one way to look at the visitations, i.e., that they are different beings who only fly here from other planets. But research into government documents, thanks to the Freedom of Information Act, that everyone so hoped would prove that other-worlders do visit, has, over the last forty-five+ years, led nowhere. For Luke, better documents for study are the biblical texts. There, he and others have found numerous descriptions of UFO/alien encounters that closely match what people have been reporting in modern times. But he does not believe anyone is coming from distant places in our Universe; rather, they may be from other dimensions.

Some of the answers are not easy, even when the ships practically land in your yard. You have to keep fishing.

Endnote

[1]While the Internet reported in 2010 that 100 million people had thus far made official reports about witnessing some form of UFO anomaly, most folk do not report their experiences. A better estimate of UFO experiencers, I believe, is around 2.5 billion!

Chapter 19

NORTH JERSEY SHORT STUFF

**Brief UFO reports courtesy of
The International UFO Museum and Research Center, Roswell, New Mexico;
the National UFO Reporting Center (www.ufocenter.com);
and Filer's Files.com**

**March 23, 2012;
no time given**

Clinton Township, Hunterdon County

It was early morning when the observer was awakened by a loud whirring sound mixed with static electricity. The noise came from outside her home. She hurried outside to investigate the clamor and was astonished by a large triangular-shaped craft hovering over a small bay on the Wolf River, just to the east of her residence. The UFO was dark with no lights and was dropping bright colored orbs over the water, each of which spun for a brief moment in mid-air, and then took off at a high rate of speed in a dozen directions. As she watched, the aircraft dropped several more orbs, which took off north, speeding upstream close to the water. The craft itself also followed this route upstream on Wolf Creek at a slow speed, flying just over the trees until it was out of her view. By her frantic call, deputies from the Clinton Township and Lebanon police departments were dispatched to the scene, but they did not witness any of the events.

Hillsborough, Somerset County

It was early morning. The two stargazers sat on their back porch watching the heavens. Suddenly, a rod-shaped object moved quickly across the sky. The silent enigma appeared both to be a solid structure, yet looked like a thin cloud layer. It was huge, the size of two quarters held at arms-length next to each other. The flying vehicle was in the southwest sky and, as it flew between Jupiter and Orion, it vanished. Afterwards, one of the stargazers reported a ringing in his ears that he feels was somehow connected to the UFO.

Jersey City, Hudson County

It was not unusual for the student of aviation to view the night sky from his Jersey City apartment window. However, this Wednesday night, he noticed a hovering airborne object over the city. It had a bright red light flashing on the bottom. With his knowledge of aircraft, he knew from first glance that this was not a plane. The object was long, metallic, and had an odd bulk to its shape. Some might have identified it as a blimp, but he was sure that it was unidentifiable, as it moved slowly across the skyline. After ten minutes, it was still in plain view. For the next hour, the craft continued progressing inland away from Jersey City, which was far too long for a blimp to hover over a city at ten o'clock at night. The flashing red light was prominent the whole time. The object must have been seen by thousands.

Lopatcong, Warren County

While gazing at a partly-cloudy sky, the observer noticed a white light moving in a circular motion. As he watched, it abruptly and sporadically changed direction and continued to do so many times. After a few minutes, the white light changed into a green color and continued in the same flying pattern. Next, the ball split into two different objects, and then into three different objects that all moved in the same pattern. Suddenly, they all vanished like magic.

Middlesex, Middlesex County

On a warm Christmas day in 2010, you might expect to see a sleigh and eight tiny reindeer appear suddenly overhead, but certainly not the holiday miracle witnessed by the observer. She was sitting on her front porch when she noticed three egg-shaped extremely bright orange, slow-moving objects in the sky. They traveled together in an arrow formation, with two just behind the lead object. Although the three UFOs were flying upwards, the woman considered them to be too close to her house and it scared her. As she watched them fly over the neighbor's house, one of the objects disappeared while the other two kept going, and then they too disappeared. In telling her friends and family about the event, naturally, everyone said she saw Santa. She knows, however, she did not.

Newark, Essex County

The birthday celebration was coming to a close. It was around 6 p.m. as the celebrant and his wife watched TV with his father, when three strange-looking lights appeared in the distance outside the living-room window. His dad immediately said that they were airplanes and nothing to be concerned about. But the witness was not convinced. He leapt to the window for a better look. Something was unusual about these lights. They were not getting any closer, and pulsated as they shifted in a triangular conveyor belt motion. As he watched, they transformed from three lights to four, then to five, and then back to three. This peculiar production lasted till 3 a.m. The next day, his wife discussed the lights with her father, a valet at the Newark International Airport. Apparently, the lights were visible from the airport, but no one was able to identify them. His father-in-law also stated that the airport had called in both FEMA and the military. No knowledge had been revealed about the investigation. The following night, the radiant phenomenon returned and the husband and wife watched them until 5 a.m. At the conclusion of the second sighting, it was like a light bulb switched off, leaving the object resembling a shiny, metal sphere floating in the sky. Although the witness was now on sky-watch, no further incidences took place for over a year. Then on Christmas Eve 2011, the lights appeared again at four o'clock in the afternoon. The lights were part of a shiny, metal sphere floating in the sky, accompanied by a saucer with two bright lights coming from the center of the craft.

October 10, 2009;
approximately 5:50 p.m.

Newton, Sussex County

As the witnesses traveled on Route 206 South, it was not unusual to see a contrail overhead. However, the driver and passenger noticed that the vehicle making the trail seemed to be a bright pink "plane." The sun was not setting yet (did not set until 6:24 p.m.), so nothing should have been pink. The smoke it was spraying was gray against the blue sky. The object was moving north, almost parallel to Route 206. It looked like a plane, but had a tall fin on top in the center of the fuselage, with several points or fins coming out of the bottom and side. To say the least, it was not conventional.

June 22, 2011;
approximately 9:15 p.m.

Roosevelt, Monmouth County

The young witness was motoring along Cedarville Road heading home, when, through the trees in the eastern sky, she glimpsed an uncanny light. At first, she thought it was the moon. Then she realized it was a gigantic flying object with four lights in a row across the front. The two lights in the middle were extra bright, like headlights, but the light from all four seemed diffused. The unearthly craft was about the size of half of a football field. It moved northwest, slower than any airplane could move, and emitted a low hum. It was like a cruise liner in the sky with one blinking red light on the bottom. As she continued to observe the device, her body began to heat up in an unnatural way. She felt hot all over. While the UFO moved ominously overhead, the heat fired her imagination, feeding her ideas of alien intervention, and she became terrified. Now panicked, she pounded the accelerator and rushed home. Once there, she woke her mother, a scientist, to show her the object looming over their neighborhood, but the sky vessel had already sailed off to points unknown.

Trenton, Mercer County

The voice did not sound human. This was not bleed-over, skip, or cell phone interference. The retired law enforcement officer working a security detail had more than twenty-five years' experience with radios, communications, and walkie-talkies. As he made his rounds, he and a co-worker at the base station overheard a brief, loud, and clear voice, cross their frequency. It was louder and stronger than the usual power output. He was familiar with different languages, and could say with certainty: the voice they heard was not made by human vocal cords. There was a guttural vowel and consonant pattern spoken at a slightly higher pitch and speed than common human language. It was eerie and unintelligible. This exchange took place when he called a spot check in over the walkie-talkie to the base station. After the base station replied back to him, both men heard six words a fraction of a second later. This interaction was perceived to be either a mocking or mimicking of the base station message because it was at the same cadence and contained the same amount of phonetic groupings. The signal was crystal clear and it boomed stronger than the normal signal strength. The retired officer was 100 yards away from the base station. Over the years he had heard many different forms of bleed-over transmissions, but all were clearly made by a human tongue. This vocalization sounded similar to a young adult female. In fact, there was a female officer working that night, but the witness knew that it was not her. To confirm their suspicion, the base operator called the female officer and queried her about making any transmissions; she had not. In addition, several other security personnel working farther away on the premises had heard nothing unusual. Nothing else was heard that night.

The retired officer was no novice when it came to unusual, beyond human experiences. Back in 1974, while delivering newspapers, he had a pre-dawn, clear-sky UFO experience. He saw a bright, white oval-shaped object hovering overhead. It was the size of a dime held at arm's length. It hovered briefly when he first spied it and then it left at the speed of a heartbeat. Later, in 1978, late one afternoon his wife observed, moving at close range over a neighbor's house, a big white slipper-shaped craft with windows. Then on November 21, 2010, in the Trenton area, while driving home around 12:15 a.m., she observed a dark silhouetted craft against the clear, starlit sky. His wife could only describe the motionless craft as being ball-shaped, attached on the end of a stick. She watched for a couple of seconds, when it took off, leaving a smoke trail behind it.

February 9, 1999;
no time given

Wanaque Reservoir, Passaic County

It soon became obvious why neighbors considered the reservoir a "hotspot" to observe outer-world crafts. It was a cold February day when the two UFO hunters visited the reservoir hoping to see something. They weren't disappointed. Soon, they witnessed two objects flying over the hill on the horizon. One was pulsating with a bronze light that changed to red as it pulsed. The lights at one point increased in intensity. The hunters sat as they watched the amazing crafts flying to and fro, and then leave. This lasted about ten minutes.

July 29, 2011;
approximately 3 a.m.

Westfield, Union County

After a sleepless night, the witness sat on his back stoop early in the morning. Suddenly, a ball of light rose above some houses in the west, directly ahead of him. It moved straight up into the sky. Living near the traffic lanes of Newark Liberty International Airport, he had seen all types of flying craft and airplanes. This was none of them. Although the witness considered himself a skeptic concerning UFOs, he used his cell phone to videotape the white ball, which was about the size of Jupiter, as it ran across the sky and down behind a tree. He also observed an oval-shaped, glowing, jellyfish object with a white bubble on top and an ellipse on the bottom. There was a red pulsing light on the bottom tip that changed colors. The object brightened and then moved out of sight behind the neighbor's roof across the street. The witness ran to his front lawn and caught sight of the object again before it totally disappeared from view. Later that day, he heard from another neighbor who saw the same object at the same time that morning.

Woodbridge, Bergen County

The witness was having a restless night. After a quick visit to the bathroom, he fell back asleep. Struggling between dream and wakefulness, consciousness slowly surfaced and with it an intense feeling of being held down. He became terrified. Someone was in the room accosting him. The sleeper tried desperately to fully wake so he could defend himself, but strangely, he could not. He tried kicking his legs at the intruder, but they barely moved and felt somewhat numb. With a dreadful effort, he tried to regain control, mentally ordering his legs to kick and his eyelids to open so he could see his stealthy assailant. Finally, his eyes sluggishly opened, as if against their will. He got his first glimpse of his surroundings. Laying on his back, his hands were being forced down against his chest by a small, dark gray being who was standing on the left side of his bed. Despite the lack of light, he could see that the being was short, around four feet tall and slender like a child, also naked and completely void of hair. He did not see any facial features. With paralyzed vocal chords, his scream died before it could be born. As he continued to struggle, his strength came back. Kicks got closer to the small creature. Then his voice returned. "Get off of me!" he shrieked in the intruder's face. Abruptly, the little being turned and awkwardly ran towards the bedroom window...and disappeared into nothingness.

Chapter 20

DOES RAIN MATTER?

Newark, Essex County

"Wisdom begins in wonder."

—*Socrates*
Greek philosopher, 5th century BCE

"What is that?" Regina asked out loud. "What is that, Mom?" her seven-year-old son asked from the back seat, the second observer of the incident.

"I don't know, Michael. Honey, can you see that?" she asked her husband, who was intent on navigating the water-soaked roadway.

"No, Reg, I can't see anything up in the air. I can barely see where I'm going."

It was 1978, a torrential spring night, around 8:30. Reggie and her family rolled along Pennsylvania Avenue, heading northeast past the Link Community School. Shopping was over and they were bound for home. Regina was in the front passenger seat.

What she saw out her side window was a large, round, white light, about as big as a quarter at arms length. The odd light was under the dripping clouds, approximately three to four thousand feet high.

Newark International Airport was only a few miles to the south. She thought at first that it was a plane flying slightly off course and too low. But this light was huge compared to a plane's light, even at close range. Besides, planes have many lights: running lights, wing lights, strobe lights. None of these were visible. And there was no noise. Airplanes create a racket wherever they go. And this one should have been extra loud due to its proximity. She could not tell how fast it was flying, or if it was moving at all.

She opened her car window for an untainted view.

Could this be a UFO, Regina wondered? It sure did not fit any other explanation. But what was it doing out in the rain? A quick scan of her memory banks revealed an absence of info about UFOs ever appearing anywhere in the rain. Maybe it was something else, like a…

Suddenly, a smaller light, about a quarter the size of the large one, shot straight out from the center of the large light like a bullet out of a Ruger pistol. The projectile-light also seemed round and zipped across the clouded sky at tremendous speed from right to left and was gone in two seconds.

"Oh, my god! Did you see that?" Regina blurted. Her list of wonderings about what the light actually could be instantly shortened. She popped her head out the window, clamping her hat down with her left hand. The hard, fast-moving rain drenched her. But she needed to hear rocket sounds and jet engines so this peculiar scenario could end based on something measurable, something earth-bound.

But she only heard the sound of falling water and traffic.

"Wow, Mommy, that was cool!" Michael had squeaked from the rear when the little light shot left.

Her husband made a couple of quick glances to the right in the hopes of being a participant in this family event, but the remaining UFO was too far to his right and too high for him to see from the busy driver's seat.

"It's probably just an airplane," he decided after not having seen anything. "Close the window, will ya?"

"It can't be a plane. Why would that light shoot out like that?" No sooner had Regina said those words than the large light vanished like a trick in a magic act.

"It's gone. Oh my god, it just disappeared! Did you…"

"No, I didn't see it," her man partially growled.

"All right, all right. Give me a minute to calm down. How high do you think these clouds are?" she asked, a partial deflection for relationship's sake. Her partner stole a couple of glimpses into the dark, wet sky.

"Can't be much more than 5,000 feet. They're gorged with water. That's why it's raining so hard," he quickly noted, proud of his amateur meteorological prowess.

"Makes sense," she agreed. "Maybe fighters from Maguire Air Force Base were over Newark firing missiles."

"What?! No way," her husband countered indignantly, as if the U.S. Air Force could never do anything wrong.

"But there was no sound. And where would the missiles land?" Regina second-guessed herself. "It would be too dangerous to practice shooting over a city, particularly in a heavy rainstorm."

"How about *way* too dangerous."

They continued home.

The light that shot across the black night from the larger light seemed intelligently motivated to Regina, like it was a planned operation. It was not a shooting star because it traveled at true horizontal, parallel to the ground. And shooting stars do not begin their journeys in the middle of a ball of light at about 4,000 feet.

That night, Regina and her family drove down the street of rained-out ideas into a future of wonderment about life in the Universe, its likelihoods and impossibilities, and the question of alien visitation.

Chapter 21

DIVINE EVIDENCE
Warren Township, Somerset County

"When the solution is simple, God is answering."

—Albert Einstein
German-born theoretical physicist

Clare was off that night. As an emergency room nurse at the local hospital, her shifts were often long and tedious, blended with frantic moments trying to ease the trauma and suffering of the unfortunate. Her life was grounded in a caregiver's reality, and not prone to fantasy.

On Sunday night, July 20, 2003, Clare motored her white Dodge Neon home from Bible study. While her faith was strong, Clare often pondered the need for belief, when proof – sometimes – seemed like an easier alternative. The Creator could easily give her the power of instant healing to truly "nurse" people to good health. But, as her minister often preached, God was not to be tested. The Divine managed "existence" on its own schedule, not Clare's. And would not such a request for a miracle, as was often taught, liken one to Satan tempting Christ in the desert? The cool July air consisted of an unpleasant paradox; "believe" without proof and be rewarded; request "knowing" via proof and be condemned. Clare's heart and mind volleyed these concepts on her spiritual court as she drove home.

It was after 9 p.m., an unremarkable calm summer night. As she was coming up the hill on Mountain Boulevard in Warren Township, she saw a huge, round, blue, with windows all around, "typical" saucer UFO. Typical to her eyes, because similar ones were plastered on TV shows like the SyFy Channel's *Ancient Aliens*, all over the Internet, and in movies like *Independence Day*. But the craft was untypical to her mind and heart, both of which sprinted off in different directions, one clamoring for logical facts and figures, the other screaming for a positive emotional/spiritual connection. Clare edged her auto to a stop on the side of the road.

Other drivers pulled over and parked, exited their vehicles and began pointing up and chatting amongst themselves. Clare found herself in the middle of a scene from a *Twilight Zone* rerun. Unlike '60s people who would have gravitated together in a large, protective group, the 21st century folk stood near their own cars, conversing amongst themselves, wondering what it was, and what it meant to them, but not involving strangers.

There were no lights on the device that Clare could see. It was approximately ten feet in diameter. The craft hovered at a flagpole's height, out of place, as if it was a forgotten prop left by the special effects department. Despite its closeness, there was no sound from the machine. In fact, nature seemed unusually still for a summer night, except for the occasional hum of a car at idle, or humans mumbling.

Clare was in awe, her jaw down about an inch from the closed position. Emotions, already in a conflict from Bible class, now swelled like the Tigris-Euphrates Rivers meeting a tsunami.

Was this disc for real? Even if it was, should she believe in it? Did its presence display a refutation of the Bible? Was the Divine happy about all this?

"What is this thing?" she wondered. But beyond that, she didn't know what to say or think. From within her shaky frame more trouble was brewing. One strong feeling swam upward through her seething sea of confusion and broke the surface.

"Am I going insane?" It was a nurse's question. Hard-won medical training suddenly formed an umbrella against surging emotions. The prognosis, however, did not look well. Most of her life Clare had been told flying devices from other places did not exist. The American government had made numerous statements to the same effect, and Christian luminaries from all sects debated against the "plurality of worlds." So how could it hang in the air in front of her in such blatant defiance?

Maybe her mind was cracking.

Massive stress in the ER, planning her upcoming wedding, constant money issues – all part of her day-to-day existence – were barriers to serenity.

The flying saucer had to be a hallucination.

While that concept solved the God/Bible/belief problem, it opened a frightening health-door. Was this sighting the onset of delirium, dementia, epilepsy, psychotic depression, kidney failure, brain cancer, or any one of various other maladies that listed hallucination as a possibility? Sets of accompanying symptoms for each disease began to tick off in Clare's head, but she cut them off. An answer was needed right now.

She could run to one of the other parked cars, slap her hands on the hood to see if it was real; shake the driver and demand to know whether they were real and whether they saw the same flying saucer as she did. But whether she perceived them as flesh and blood or not, and no matter what their answer, it could all be part of the same illusion. There was only one person she could trust.

Her fiancé, Jason, lived a couple miles away.

Five minutes had passed since she first saw the peculiar saucer.

Vaulting into the car, Clare banged her head on the door frame, then banged the shifter into gear while hitting the gas, screeching the front tires into an action that shot the four cylinders swerving down the street.

Within moments, she was at Jason's house, dragging him down the walkway and into the Neon, half against his will, to experience something wonderful; his first UFO encounter – or not. Clare thought at the moment that she would be happy either way.

But when they returned to the scene, the UFO had vanished. The autos and their occupants who had been there watching along with her were also gone. Mountain Boulevard was empty, quiet, as if nothing exciting had happened there in a thousand years. It had barely been ten minutes since Clare had left a would-be spaceship hovering overhead, got her boyfriend, and returned. The entire episode, so real at first, now implied: mirage. Clare was embarrassed. Despite her fiancé's guarantee of his belief in her experience, there was nothing tangible, nor remnant – like a few of the earlier witnesses still hanging around that they could talk to – to convince her that he was convinced. A darkened dreamscape was beginning to envelope the event in her mind. It drew into question her mental health.

She drove Jason home, and then hastened herself to her own bed for a night of endless tossing and turning.

Early the next morning, her cell phone beeped her awake. It was her girlfriend, Sandy.

"You're never gonna guess what I saw last night?" her friend jabbered through the tiny speaker.

Clare's first want was to challenge that question with her own paranormal experience. But fear of rejection, belittlement, even condemnation, kept her response common.

"Okay, I give up already. What did you see?"

"I saw a real, live, flying saucer! It was over Mountain Boulevard. Had to be around ten o'clock or so. I was on my way home from Mom's…" The rest of the conversation comprised of small *ohs* and *ahs* from Clare, which were all she could muster, as Sandy revealed in detail that exact flying ship that Clare had watched only an hour earlier than her dear friend.

"I saw the same thing around 9!" Clare finally screamed into the phone.

"Oh my god!" Sandy gasped, and the two women compared every detail of the two sightings.

Relief sprang anew for Clare. Corroboration had come, and faith in her own sensibilities was secure. She and her friend had shared a miracle. And they could talk about it whenever they wished.

There is so much of our little Universe that we have no experience with, why would anyone think that we were the only ones in that enormous space? The Divine created the 50,000,000,000,000,000,000,000 stars (that's 50 sextillion, a minimum estimate) in the universe with an inestimable number of planets circling them. So why not create other beings besides us? Everything that comes our way is evidence of the divine design, something so beyond human experience and imagination that seeing the pattern is impossible. Our minds are finite, timed-out with death, so that we cannot grasp the infinite and eternal empire.

All of this is confirmed by the simple presentation of a flying machine from out of this world.

Chapter 22

GREEN BACKS
Long Branch, Monmouth County

"Appearances are a glimpse of the unseen."

—Anaxagoras
Greek Philosopher, 5th century BCE

"You're green!" both mother and son shouted to each other; the four-year-old son blurted as if some Christmas-like celebration was ready to start; Erin, his mother, gasped as if the world had been dyed by the blood of a giant Japanese movie monster.

June 30, 1983 was supposed to be like any other Thursday. And it had been up until dusk. Erin had fixed breakfast, lunch, and dinner for her four-year-old, Jimmy, bought groceries and gas for the car, mailed a package at the post office, and purchased two quarts of light blue paint at the hardware store for the bathroom project. The afternoon saw a couple hours of play on the beach at their favorite spot just south of McLoon's Pier House and a stroll on Long Branch's boardwalk.

Erin's house, an older, two-story, wood-framed single, faced Edwards Avenue and was bordered by a rivulet of the Branchport Creek in back. Jimmy's bedroom on the second floor overlooked the small stream that his mother forbade him to play near.

As the day receded, hopes for an average night abated with equal swiftness.

The sky was clean and clear. The last of the sunshine was deflected by distant buildings and tree lines. Eight-thirty had approached faster than calculated and that meant only one thing for Jimmy: bath time and then bed.

Between a brief phone call and playtime in the tub, Erin finally got her offspring scraped and polished and laying on his bed. She shuffled through his dresser for matching pajama tops and bottoms, which she thought would be easy since she had arranged the drawer. But the mischief maker in the room must have dove in during some imaginary adventure searching for treasure and did an Atlantic City-job of shuffling the contents. The light from the hall poured into the open bedroom doorway with sufficient incandescence.

Suddenly, everything turned green.

Erin looked instinctively over her shoulder. Jimmy was laying on his tummy, studying his Obi-Wan Kenobi action figure. He, in turn, flipped his head left to see his mom.

Their backs and everything else in the room were a dull green.

Erin flashed a gaze to the only window in the room. The normal view of Monmouth Racetrack and beyond were gone. In its stead was a powerful green light shooting into the entire room like a laser, replacing all other colors as if a dark lime sun had risen in front of the glass.

Mother and son looked at each other again.

"You're green!" they yelled in unison.

Shock and disquiet filled Erin's being, but curiosity overthrew both and pressed her forward with three fast steps to the window. There was something there; the light was coming from...

Then it was gone.

In one second, the green light source whisked away off into the northern sky and vanished, and with it went the emerald glow.

Erin flipped up the screen window and stuck her head outside to get a parting view of whatever it was that had blasted them with verde. Too late. The troublemaker had fled like a neighborhood brat caught in the act of peeping.

Never again did Erin witness the paranormal. Never did she need to. The memory of the brazen green color, so near and so intense, so renovating of an entire room in an instant, is deeply burned into her mind.

It is the first image she has when topics of "strange phenomenon" emerge in conversations.

It is the last color she would ever use in her house.

Chapter 23

ROUTE 579 TRIO

Ringoes, Hunterdon County
by Gerard J. Medvec

"Actions are always more complex and nuanced than they seem. We have to be willing to wrestle with paradox in pursuing understanding."

—*Harold Evans*
British-born journalist, writer, editor

One hundred yards off the driver's side of the car were three beautiful probes of alien inquiry.

It was a clear night on January 18, 2013, and the ride from Delaware City, Delaware, up to Ringoes, New Jersey, had been turn-filled, yet uneventful. I was looking forward to the 7:30 p.m. meeting with the UFO group there. As always, between defensive driving and following my handwritten directions during the two-hour trip, I was searching for UFOs.

To label the process of looking for space-brothers as "UFO hunting" is common. But it dawned on me recently that "hunting" is an ignominious term. There was no hunting to be done. I carried no guns, hauled no cage, nor did I set any traps – as if the aliens would permit their own capture or demise with such primitive pieces of junk. The process has now been relabeled as "watching." It feels better, student-like, even friendly. I'm hoping that the aliens will take that as a sign of growth and be more open to my presence and allow me a bigger part in their program, perhaps an honorary membership.

But maybe direct participation in an alien civilization is not the best wish in the genie's lamp.

Throughout my sixty years, the idea of "joining" has been an issue. Off again, on again, as I've matured into various areas of personality, so has my interest in becoming part of a group. Through my teens and twenties, I refused to join anything. No team, no religion, no after-work-group, no association, no anything interested me enough to elicit a commitment.

Then in my late thirties and early forties, I joined over a half-dozen different groups: four different fraternities, two religions, and two work-related organizations. But by the time my late forties came, I had quit all but one of them. Now at sixty, I belong to three groups, two of which are UFO organizations in Philadelphia and New York City. There was nothing wrong with those other institutions. Their merits were far flung and in some cases world renown, but each of them suffered from a flaw that permeates all human collectives: the regularly scheduled meeting.

Of course, meetings are good from time to time. Often they are mandatory in order to coalesce information or come to a final decision on some important issue. Finding like-minds on a given topic is comforting, and making contacts is important; the chance to make good acquaintances or even a new close friend is even better.

In my opinion, however, more often than not, the "regular meeting" is unnecessary. Much time is wasted talking about "what was" rather than using that same time to take an action. And to me, with UFOs, action is awesome! It's great that so many UFO investigators are looking into experiences that people claim to have with the paranormal, but really, it's all after the fact. The investigator was not present during the experience, so he/she becomes dependent upon residual evidence and testimony. This type of evidence can only ever lead to circumstantial proof. In the realm of the paranormal, there is only one proof: your own firsthand experience. Seeing a ghost or a UFO with your own eyes is a game-changing, life-enhancing incident. Impact of such an event on an individual is beyond measurement. Sorry, the scientific method does not apply here, since it is limited to empirical three-dimensional processes. Aliens are not inclined to submit to our examination, and their crafts and devices are too fast to get a tape-measure on them. The only proof of the UFO phenomenon will be when the American government admits that they are here, or that the aliens themselves make some worldwide revelation. Neither of these proclamations seems likely soon.

Back to the meeting; it started promptly, ran efficiently, was exuberant, and I had a good time. One thing perplexed me, however, at its very beginning. When I asked the five local members if there was any UFO activity in that precise neighborhood, I was told "no." One person had lived in the area for fourteen years and had never seen any alien stuff.

This region was a beautiful rural Jersey setting. There were small, open, rolling foothills that worked their way northward towards the greater Appalachians. The land was dotted by houses, with occasional sections combed into rows of a plowed field. Set away from any great city, the area was inviting, dark, and a perfect spot for UFO shenanigans.

"I'm surprised to hear there is no activity here," I commented after getting the bad news. "This, to me, is just the kind of place I would come to watch for UFOs." The subject was then dropped; the meeting progressed through an informative two hours.

Soon enough, because of this light exchange of ideas, I would be questioning my sanity.

After leaving the meeting, I began retracing the semi-complicated journey towards Delaware. At that early stage of the trip, I was more concerned about finding my way out of Ringoes and back to Route 295 south, so I could put my mind on cruise-control and enjoy a straight-forward drive home. Reading the directions backwards was holding my attention.

I had only gone about two miles when I crossed Toad Road on Route 579 heading south. It was around 10:45 p.m.

Suddenly, about 1,000 feet past the intersection, on the left in an open field, something grabbed my attention.

"What the heck is that?" To my amazement, there were three alien globes floating above the ground.

Each of the three globes had different light-intensity and slightly different colors, though they still resembled human-made lights. They sat about 100 yards apart, about 75 to 100 feet in front of the line of trees that followed the old railroad tracks at the back of the field. This put the globes about 1,000 feet from the street. Beyond the tree line (I learned the next day via satellite map) were a few houses.

There was no pull-off on that part of Route 579 so I jerked my car into someone's driveway and shut off the engine. The lights in the house were off, so I figured there were a few minutes to witness the alien visions before being recognized as a trespasser. This position was directly across from the center globe.

I stepped behind my auto, so any traffic could slip by without stress, and stood with a good view, since the field across the street rose only four feet above the road, and I am six feet tall. The globes hovered three to four feet over the dirt, made their standard nervous short shifts back and forth, up and down, never remaining still. This movement is one of their giveaways. Seeing different intensities and colors in three probes all in the same general area was rare. Most times when there has been more than one globe floating together, they have all been the same color. Don't know why these were different. One thing was certain: the lights were not from the houses beyond the field. There is a heavy line of tall evergreens that run the entire length of the back of the field, starting in the southeast and heading northwest. Any lights from the houses would have been diffused or splintered by the thick branches and would have reached my eyes as mere glimmers. But even that did not happen, or was not noticed, due to the clear intensity of the three obvious alien devices in the forefront.

Several cars passed by in both directions along the lonely highway. Certainly any one of them could have looked to the field and seen the same round glowing images that I saw, but no one stopped. It would have been nice if they had at least slowed and called out their window to ask about my well-being since my car's flashers were blinking. Perhaps one of the UFO-meeting attendees would roll along, see me, see the globes, and stop to corroborate the experience. The best sighting is when there is more than one witness.

No luck on any front.

Ten minutes sailed by quickly and there was an hour and a half ride home ahead of me, so I reluctantly lumbered behind the wheel and started off, happy for having another alien globe incident.

But within a couple minutes, the irksome intelligence and unexplainable beauty of the UFO balls began to haunt me.

Ten minutes of view time was not enough.

I turned the car around via another driveway and headed back. Maybe I wanted to make sure the wild oddity of seeing not one, but three alien probes after a "UFO meeting" where I was assured there were no UFOs in the neighborhood, was not all invented in my otherwise not-to-inventive imagination.

The car braked to a stop across from where I had parked earlier and, thankfully, the three globes were still shining bright. Again I exited and stood in front of the car, looking from one bright ball to the next, trying to estimate distances, wondering about their origins, and hoping for some sort of impromptu aerial display or mother ship rescue mission. Maybe this would be the big moment when I would run across the thickly raised rows of dirt, throw my coat over the nearest globe, and take it home with me. No. Not that night either. Too frightened; "Need back-up," I kept telling myself.

Again, more cars sauntered by. No one stopped. No one asked, "Are you alright?" The three probes stayed focused on their work, and they made no acknowledgement of me either. It was one of those times I had wished that I had punched the phone number of the UFO group's leader into my cell phone so I could have called and screamed about the UFOs down the street from her house. I was just getting into that habit whenever I headed for a new destination to put in my contact's number in the cell phone. Why I forgot it that night was uncertain and a little irritating.

Another ten minutes washed away from my life watching the strange visitors from a strange place, and the tug from home grew stronger. It was time to go.

This was sighting number twenty-three for me. I started keeping count when contracts to write UFO books fell into my lap. Some people think twenty-three is an impossibly high count; for others, it pales against their own claims. I'm happy with it. I know they are real.

The drive home consisted of black coffee, big band music, and constant scanning of the skies and darkened-off road areas for alien anything. But no more was to be seen that night and the adventure was over.

In regards to action, I have wondered what effect an "Appeal to the Aliens Day" would bring. Everyone on Earth would go outside and yell all at once for the aliens to make their presence known...and then wait to see what happens. It would be embarrassing if it worked; a child-like strategy that beat out the SETI program that spent millions each year for over forty-years with zero results. I wish it would happen, but I don't know how to organize it.

But I had my own embarrassment to contend with. There are no UFOs in the neighborhood, but I saw three.

It was only right (I thought) to contact the UFO group the next day and tell folk about what I saw. The closer I came to punching the first phone number, however, the more reticent I felt.

Does it not seem odd, I believed the lady leading the group would think that I came all the way from Delaware for a two-hour meeting and then "miraculously" see three alien probes on the way home? And only two miles from the meeting house, when people had openly explained that there was no activity in the area? What are the chances? If I did see something, it must be that I'm either fabricating or a marked person and that the aliens send devices that are for my eyes only.

The problem with these "feelings" from other people is that they imply I am a liar or I am special.

I am neither.

Anyone who drove along Route 579 that night at approximately 10:45 p.m. and looked into that field would have seen three "lights." But would it have dawned on any of them that they were not human-made? That they were from somewhere else performing some completely incomprehensible project known only to an other-worldly species?

Probably not. Why would they? Most folk are totally wrapped up in their societally induced and self-inflicted life complications.

Yet people did drive by that night while I stood in the street gazing hard at the field, enamored with the floating globes.

Nobody stopped; uninterested in anything but their destination, too tired after a day of meetings, I guess.[1]

Endnote

[1] For an example of my showing a stranger real "alien activity" and the amusing end result, read *UFOS Above PA*, Chapter 16 "Alien Base Camp."

Chapter 24

AMWELL ROAD
Somerset, Somerset County

"I am free because I know."

—*Robert A. Heinlein*
American science fiction writer

"Holy hell, holy hell, holy hell! That's a UFO!" Jimmy's first-time view of alien aircraft rattled his intestines down to the spiritual level.

On April 4, 2005, Jimmy's normal near-dawn start at his dry-cleaning company was waylaid by an appointment his wife had with the family doctor. By the time he dropped her back off at their home in Flemington, it was well past one o'clock. Though he did not need to take the hour ride into New Brunswick, he felt some important paperwork could be handled, and a part-day at work was better than no-day. Besides, an odd feeling nagged him to go. Maybe some unknown problem was about to erupt and his presence would resolve it. So he motored off to New Brunswick.

He shot the car along Route 514, also known as Amwell Road, wondering how to improve dry-cleaning turn-over, how to pay various invoices in the 30-60-90-day files, and how to handle that one trouble-making employee.

Around 2 p.m., he coasted to a halt at a traffic light turned red. This was at the T-intersection of Amwell Road and Cedar Grove Lane in Somerset, New Jersey. Jimmy waited to turn right onto Cedar Grove. The sky was a beautiful clear blue with no clouds and the sun was directly behind him lighting up the Mobile station (in 2013 CE, it is a Shell Gas Station) directly across the street. Jimmy was first in line at the intersection, so nothing blocked his view of the majestic firmament.

Ticking off the seconds for the light to change, he gazed up with vacant contentment at his favorite color, sky blue.

To his shock, the color chip-solid heavens were precipitously interrupted by a cigar-shaped tube seeming to hover motionless directly above the gas station across the street. It was not there a second earlier. Where had it come from?

Seconds passed as his mind processed the peculiar shape that seemed uploaded onto his view screen (windshield) from some dastardly malware. Something felt odd. Why couldn't he recognize this thing? He knew what airplanes and helicopters, dirigibles, balloons, birds, fireworks, arrows, kites, Frisbees, rockets, javelins, baseballs, trapeze artists, and dozens of other things that moved briefly through the air looked like. Since he had been waiting all his fifty years to see an actual UFO, what was the hold-up in the I.D. department?

Then, like a football coach doused by icy water after a win, the realization of the uniqueness of the metal tube hovering ahead of him soaked into every cell of his being. The craft matched nothing Jimmy had ever seen before on Earth.

"Holy hell, holy hell, holy hell! That's a UFO!" he yelled out loud, bouncing the excitement off the windshield and back into his own ears.

Mental notes of the UFO's visual details scribbled across pages of his mind. The color was a dull white. No gleaming or reflection even though the sun was shining directly on it; "classic" cigar-shaped. No windows or markings. No wings, fins, tail, or obtrusions of any type. No exhaust trail. No noise. In fact, the object made no sense at all. It looked like metal, therefore, heavy. No propulsion system appeared in use, let alone evident, so the whole thing should have crashed like a lead zeppelin.

Like any guy, Jimmy tended to measure sizes and distances against dimensions he knew well: fifteen feet from the foul line to a basketball hoop, 100 yards (300 feet) for the length of a football field. The height of the ship from the ground was about two football fields, about 600 feet. The distance from his seat in the car to directly below the object was about 450 feet. He quickly shot his index finger up at arm's length and the UFO was close to covered by it.

Finally, he felt he had some facts, diminutive, but real.

Before the traffic light changed green, the UFO started to drift right towards JFK Boulevard, about two miles east. When the light went green, Jimmy turned right and drove parallel to the white tube, concentrating half on traffic, half on the miracle in the sky coasting outside his driver's window.

Then it began accelerating, as if intentionally thwarting close scrutiny. Tree lines came and went, hiding, then revealing the craft like a game of peek-a-boo.

Was anyone else on Amwell Road seeing this? Plenty of cars were behind him and oncoming, but none dashed to the roadside, no one was pointing up beyond their windows. It seemed like an average day on the average street. Jimmy knew better.

Happily, a great confirmation flew his way, a direct and instant comparison between the UFO and "two of ours." Two commercial jet airliners were flying directly across the windshield, right to left. Clearly their wings, tails, windows, and logo markings were visible, despite their higher altitudes. This gave him total conviction that what he saw and described was an actual UFO.

By the time he arrived at the intersection of Amwell Road and JFK Boulevard, the UFO was speeding away towards Easton Avenue, a more northern direction and out of following range.

Jimmy barged into his buzzing dry-cleaner shop by 2:15 p.m. and told the employees, "I think I just saw a UFO." They knew of his belief in extraterrestrials through occasional break-time conversations.

Now that speculation for Jimmy was over and firsthand experience was in place, would they believe him?

He was never sure. Maybe they did not want to believe; maybe they could not. Once in his office, he called his wife and filled her in. She was accepting. As that day whisked by, he remained excited about the white tube. This prompted him into a new wave of UFO book and article reading and TV viewing. Soon after, he joined a local UFO group where he is still engaged.

Looking back, he was not sure why he told his employees, "I think I just saw a UFO," because he *knew* he had seen a UFO, and was revved-up for the next one.

Chapter 25

OUTER VALENTINE
Elizabeth, Union County

"There is nothing worse than a sharp image of a fuzzy concept."

—Ansel Adams
American photographer and environmentalist

Out of the fog, the blinking lights shot towards the balcony as fast as phaser fire. Liz panicked backwards. She bounced off the sliding glass door of her fifth-floor apartment and lurched towards the metal railing with a sixty-foot drop beyond. She stiffened her frightened arms and hand-locked the cold handrail, stopping forward motion.

There in front of her was the source of the lights: a menacing black triangle as quiet as an infant's sleep, hanging off the balcony like a still-life only two feet from her face.

It was February 13, 1984, a foggy, windless winter evening with temperatures in the forties, making Elizabeth, New Jersey balmy.

Liz got home near the usual 7 p.m. from her family service counselor's job at the funeral home on Elizabeth Avenue. Constantly ribbed about seeing "dead people," she actually never did; unless one considered the grieving relatives as people bordering on death-by-misery. Bodies went directly into the preparation room and Liz never attended the funerals. They made her queasy. Yet her sales figures were high, thanks to ad-on services and refineries she recommended to the grieving family to "enhance the dignity of the occasion."

Beating up heart-broken relatives about spending more money than necessary on funeral arrangements was accomplished, she acknowledged, through a toughened heart. Liz did not realize at the time, unfortunately, that a hard heart would shed pain and love equally well.

Not that UFOs cared. Whether the visiting craft near the balcony knew Liz was dateless the next night for Valentine's Day or not, it seemed determined to cut-in with its own agenda.

The high-rise apartment building near the corner of North Street and N. Broad Street in Elizabeth made the perfect setting. The fifth-floor balcony looked due south. It served two adjacent apartments, but was divided in half by a masonry wall for privacy. Someone on the balcony could be quite alone, and nothing would obstruct a small flying machine from visiting the entire side of the building, doubly so in fog.

Taking a fifth-floor dwelling had been an imposing and involuntary choice for Liz.

She was afraid of heights. Not only high heights, like a thousand feet or so, but any dimension a couple of inches or more off the ground.

She had applied for a one-bedroom unit on the ground floor first, but took too long to shop it and lost it to a quicker renter. Time had pressed her since the lease on her old apartment was expiring and most other living quarters she looked at were unacceptable. So she signed for the fifth floor two-bedrooms with a balcony she would never use.

Not exactly.

Walking up and down stairs was disquieting for Liz even when the staircase was tightly enclosed. The sight of steps, escalators, or ladders twisted her tummy into a sailor's knot. Yet, she had to live. Moving up and down inside buildings for a city/suburbanite was mandatory. Deep breaths and eyes level, looking neither up nor down, got her through the day. One of the perks at the funeral home was her first-floor office.

The N. Broad Street apartment had one saving factor that helped Liz past her fear. There was an elevator. It buffered the perception of height so her trips to the fifth became simply: walk to the elevator, door open, door close, sensation of movement, door open, walk down hall to apartment door. It felt fine. The staircases from basement to rooftop, however, which she only saw once during the tour of the property, felt dizzying. The narrow six-inch gap past the railings threatened to yank her feet downward, though in reality, she would never fit. Likewise, looking up the tower caused vertigo. In 1984, she had been there four years.

The night before Valentine's Day had been a normal one for Liz. By the time she ate, got an outfit ready for the following day's work, watched TV, and read part of a crime novel in bed, the clock approached midnight.

Ready to close the book and hit the lights, something urged her to go to the kitchen. She told herself she was thirsty. A drink of water would be nice. But it wasn't true.

She hopped from bed in her flannel pajamas, slipped on her slippers, and shuffled out of the bedroom. But rather than dart for the drink, she slid towards the balcony off the dining area and threw back the sheer white curtains, something she never did, and did not know why she did now.

Everything was light gray, the fog thick enough to block all views in every direction removing the sense of up and down and giving the illusion of a solid wall at the end of the balcony.

This surprised the occupant and curiosity drew her towards the edge. Traffic from the popular intersection at the corner was still faintly heard most nights even at a late hour. But this night it contained no noise, save for her banging heart, reminding her of her height-fear.

Solid fog smelled like a damp cloth. The sky was soothing and blank and...

"What's that?" she asked no one.

As Liz gazed about, she saw above her, at about forty-five degrees, at an indeterminate distance, three white lights in a triangle formation. "What is that?" she wondered aloud to the deep smoke as she stepped back from the railing.

The lights changed position. The "lead" light had been pointing left. Now the three wavering bulbs shifted in unison, putting the front light aiming at her building like an electric arrowhead.

Liz could not tell how far up the lights were, but she believed no more than a couple floors above her.

More than that, something disturbed her. The lights having moved in unison said that they were all connected somehow. Apparently, they were attached to the same object.

"That's not a plane or helicopter," she realized, knowing well the tell-tale signs of human craft, having lived her entire life in the flight paths of Newark International Airport, just four miles northeast of Elizabeth. The intense quiet confirmed her feelings that these lights were way outside any human box since humans can do few things quietly – certainly not in the realm of airships since it takes violent, noisy power to keep them aloft.

Smoke flowed eerily over the aerial bulbs. Mesmerized, Liz scrapped rust from the dark edges of her mind in search of an explanation for the vision above her.

A litany of what the lights were not began rolling through her head when...

One second. In one second, the three globes dropped from several stories up to level with Liz's eyes and within two feet of her nose.

It was a small craft, a triangle. At close range, it was blacker than three a.m. Liz saw that it was approximately twelve feet long on each edge, about eight inches in height, a blue haze emitting all around, no lights on the sides or top that she could perceive (she could not see the back edge), and dead silent. The leading point was softly rounded and the whole thing either gave off a slight whiff of smoke, or it had dragged some of the fog along with it, Liz could not tell. Most important, it seemed to be looking at her.

All this was noticed, despite the vehicle's onrush, causing Liz's instant repel to the patio door and rebound towards the railing-precipice. Breaths were short, tight, terror-filled. What was this thing? Who sent it? Liz did not believe in UFOs and though she had not had time to complete her "what-it-is-not" survey, she was convinced that other-worldly ships would be first on that list in the u-section.

"It does look alien," she thought, tempted to reach out and touch the surface.

But when completing that idea, the ship began to move.

It rose slowly, straight up, enwrapping itself in the cloud-blanket that surrounded the building. Liz leaned over the balcony to watch, like an eager child searching for Santa. From that angle, she noticed the rear edge of the machine bent inward at the center giving the overall appearance of a cubist-painter's heart. When the machine reached the apparent top of the building, the now tiny lights disappeared over the roof.

It was getting away. While Liz was not thrilled to experience whatever this thing was, be it person-made or otherwise; she was also unwilling to let go of it without more explanation, more information so answers would be gleaned.

Liz charged through the apartment, knocking over the lamp her mother had given her, out the front door to the elevator, her only hope. Her right index finger machine-gunned the up button. But the lighted panel above the door said the elevator was in the lobby.

Too long. There was no time.

Around the corner from the lift she ran, through the stairwell door. Liz cursed to herself as the door slammed behind her, bellowing an echo through the stairwell.

The longest three seconds of her life began.

Wild fear filled her as she looked up and down the staircase, a structure she had avoided all her life. Traveling the stairs threatened her psyche. The next breath jammed in her windpipe refusing to move up or down. Senses tried to convince her that she stood atop Mt. McKinley, poised for a head-long dive to her death. Legs and arms quavered as the second hand on the watch she wore all day and night, ground from one moment to the next.

She began to march.

Was this all worth it? She did not know why, but she needed to continue.

Sweat began beading, then dripping off her forehead as nausea attacked. Legs that were used to wall-to-wall carpeting, occasional dancing, and short walks from parking lots, though shapely, instantly rebelled with pain against the five-story uphill climb. Still they pressed on, partly on Liz's command, partly against her will. Something compelled her beyond common reasoning to mount the building, to take a lunatic's stand unprotected atop a ten-story structure at night, and to follow her new metallic heart that floated outside her body wherever it went. The memory of the heart-shaped triangle poked through the fear, reminding her that something important might be waiting on the roof. Maybe the door at the top of the stairs would be open, maybe not. Maybe it would open, or lock-out, a revelation. But nothing further could be gained, and the satisfaction of having tried would be lost, as long as she remained frozen on the sixth-floor landing. She needed to move.

Time clutched at her throat and slapped her into urgency. How long would a UFO wait for someone? "Not at all," she suddenly gasped aloud. She began to run, pulling at the railing, hauling her weight against nasty gravity, determined for unknown reasons to do something no one had business doing. Then, a mistake. She looked down into the gap between the stairs. Her body rattled with shivers. She flung herself against the outside wall, feet moving ever upwards, determined. She ran, straining her body against years of sedentary disuse, powering up the steps, bouncing on and off the outside walls, keeping as far from the gap in the center of the stair shaft as possible.

Up the next four floors without camera or any thought to technology she raced. The need was for physical contact, not electronic proof. Unused to immediate bursts of hard running, her lungs pounded out a quickening rhythm that burned the inside of their pleura, and her heartbeat leapt from funeral march to rock solo. By the ninth floor, calves and thighs felt like they were being pan-seared. Sweat rolled from beneath medium length brown hair in continuous drops.

She approached the exit door to the roof.

"Be open, be open," she demanded and begged in equal pants, since the logic of the moment would fizzle if she were left stranded, propped against cold steel with a tired, dizzying decent next on her to-do list – and all for nothing.

Just before reaching it, Liz heard the door make a metallic sound on its own.

"Did that damn door just lock itself?" she wondered, thinking some advanced laser security system was tripped to lock her off the roof. But there was no such system.

She hit the long brass bar that activated the release with her remaining might.

The door swung fast and wide into the cool night air.

More profound ten-stories up, stillness was everywhere. The plush fog maintained the illusion of a solid roof and walls surrounding the apartment house, as though a building within a building.

And there, head-high over the middle of the roof, was the black craft, motionless, quiet. It was beautiful in its simplicity and powerful in its effortlessness. And Liz could feel that it had waited for her. Her heart was suddenly awash in love, a strange, mental-spiritual love that description surrendered over. This feeling of affection was new to her, perhaps new to anyone, similar to romantic and filial love, but in a broader range and intensity. And she knew it made no sense for her to experience it.

The triangle-heart tilted about twenty degrees to her right, then straightened again. And she realized it was not a tilt, it was a nod, a tip of the hat from a foreign gentleperson. A half-smile broke her lips.

Then it was gone.

Up in a perfect vertical line, it shot into oblivion is less than a second, done without sound and without atmospheric turbulence, leaving Liz surround by her feelings and a gentle cloud covering.

She looked at her watch. It was 12:01 a.m., Valentine's Day.

Could the tryst with the strange machine and the feelings of caring qualify as a date? It was another impossibility that she would later try to justify in the retelling of her blurry, off-the-wall tale – a tale of a mysterious flying craft, of conquering one's fears, and of receiving a strange Valentine, all during only a few minutes of life. It was a story that she barely believed and that no one else would believe for over twenty years.

The next day, Liz told her family of the weird event, but met with powerful resistance. Her mother said she was crazy and needed psychiatric help, a boyfriend, a new job, or all of the above. Later, friends would also scoff. Liz never broached the subject with any of them again.

The image that she remembers is crystal clear, but the idea of a smartly controlled flying machine leaves her staggering. Still uncertain of what happened that night, she is clear on a few points: one, it did happen; two, she was conscious the whole time; and three, she will never forget it.

Liz's unexpected suitor that night did something that recent human suitors met over the romantically dull previous four years did not do: it brought urgent excitement to the table. Liz could not figure out if it was the negotiating table, the examining table or what, but she is pleased that no table was apparent in the end. She was also glad that no further sightings of mist-shrouded phenomenon interrupted her evenings.

Despite that, her outlook on life altered a substantial bit over the next few months. But crediting the nebulous concept of alien life for the changes, Liz is unwilling to do.

While her sales numbers at work continue to shine, her approach to helping the bereaved softened. She modified what could have been taken for as manipulation and warmed it into real concern. Also, her relaxed attitude and increased openness may have led to her meeting a wonderful man shortly after the UFO sighting, whom she eventually married. The two professionals lived in Liz's apartment, shared the bills, and found lots of time to dance and travel. Her hubby was a believer in UFOs and the two read and watch everything in the media about the topic, growing from people of casual interest to dedicated experts.

Actively searching for alien life as it visits planet Earth is not a compelling drive for Liz. She likes her books, TV, and magazines accompanied by hot coffee.

The couple have remained in the same apartment ever since, happily grown older together, lived through recessions, wars, and one complete building renovation.

And, every once in a while, Liz takes the stairs.

Chapter 26

FRONT PAGE
Clark, Union County

"Where there is an open mind, there will always be a frontier."

—Charles Kettering
American inventor, engineer, businessman

As a story builder (newspaper reporter) and word sculptor (editor), Bob considered himself a trained observer. This made him a disbeliever in UFOs, magic, ghosts, or anything outside the three-dimensional world because he had never seen them. He maintained a rock-centered skepticism about most things until they were proven, especially in the case of little green men.

But in early November of 1979, Bob and his wife, Carol, would have their earthy pragmatism upended like a tectonic shift and merrily transformed into fairy dust.

The couple had attended a theatrical performance at the Ritz Theatre in Elizabeth, New Jersey. They were driving home to the southwest end of Union County, immersed in a debate over the merits of the entertainment. It was approximately 11 p.m. Since there was no alcohol at the affair, and since he and his wife did not take drugs, Bob had no excuse for what happened next. Carol had just finished her pros about the show and Bob was winding up with his cons when he was interrupted.

"That can't be a plane," his wife interjected with a calm that masked deep disquiet. Bob's foot hopped off the accelerator.

He and his wife had grown up in the suburbs of Newark, accustomed to seeing numerous types of aerial phenomena in and around Newark International Airport. They had seen everything that was to be seen in all seasons of the year, at all times of day and night. It was a busy sky.

They were about ten miles southwest of the airport.

Bob peered out the windshield across Carol's field of view. It was a crisp, windless

November evening, cloudless to a fault. He fully expected her vision to be an airplane, even though she said it was not. Carol was level-headed with good eyesight. For her to say an object was not a plane deserved investigation. She also did not say it was a helicopter, or blimp, or something recognizable. Most disturbing was the way she said "it can't be a plane." It was as if she already knew what it was, and was not happy about it.

Then Bob saw it.

It was a perfect, equilateral triangle moving slowly through the air. In contrast to the surrounding light pollution from the heavily populated Union County, the triangle was deeply dark.

Bob's eyes enlarged to the popping point. He instantly knew that he had never seen anything before like this object. Despite the shock to his system, he pulled off the road at the first opportunity to capture a better view.

He shoved the gearshift into park, got into a brief debate with Carol about her staying put for safety reasons, and jumped out of the car, leaving the door open. He needed a detailed look at the weird object. He was already thinking second- or third-page news.

The rural-suburban neighborhood had few houses and cars around. In fact, Bob's was the only car on the road at the moment. No other vehicles came by during the incident.

For some people, caution might have prevailed when leaping towards the unknown, but as a young reporter, the story meant more than the risk.

He had a clear look at the triangle. It was moving, firstly, in dead silence; secondly, the quality of its motion was unlike anything that had ever moved through the sky, and near impossible to describe. His best guess was that it was gliding rather than flying.

Along with these two incredible physicalities, the object was also moving too slow for normal aircraft needing aerodynamic assistance. He quickly made a fist and held his right arm out toward the object to see how it compared to the size of his closed hand. The triangular craft fitted nicely within the circumference of the fist, making its overall size approximately, huge. There were points of light at the apices defining its shape. But the most surprising feature was that stars were visible through the body of the machine. As the craft moved, so the stars drifted in and out of its triangle-frame.

Was this a true physical object, or was it a projection, a hologram? Or was it visiting from another dimension, simply "poking its head" into ours, doing a brief look-see to check on our progress, and the semi-transparency of the ship was the most he would see?

Continuing its slide through the air, the UFO headed northeast at a slow constant pace until it was out of Bob's sight. About five minutes had passed.

His feelings quickly changed from exuberance to paranoia. What had seemed like a great newspaper story, now felt like a dime store novel. *Why would we make an airplane shaped like a triangle? How did it move without jet engines or propellers, or noise for that matter? When did we start making airplanes so big?* More technical questions battered his brain, but one statement stabbed at his heart and took precedent over all else: the whole thing felt wrong.

Legs and feet that had bounced him out of his car moments ago became elephantine as he lumbered backwards. A liquid nitrogen-chill flowed over his spine as he fell in his seat, leaned halfway over to Carol and whispered loudly. "Don't talk about this to anybody." His face read an intensity that was midstream in evaluating the outcome of wild information spilled into the ears of disbelievers. "We'll talk about it later."

The remaining five-minute ride home was in excruciating silence. Bob's mind raced through a maze of possible words he could use to report/share/explain the impossible flying machine to the newspaper/family/police. He could tell that his wife's need to talk, stymied for the moment, bubbled inside her like a geyser building towards eruption.

Once in the family kitchen, Bob asked Carol to get a piece of paper and write about what she saw, including a drawing. He would do the same and they would compare notes and images. The test would eliminate their own unwitting collaboration when sharing the story verbally, and spotlight deadly bursts of embellishments. They finished and swapped papers.

It was immediately clear that both had seen the same flying geometric anomaly.

With both on the same page, Bob decided to contact the local police.

"Good evening, officer. I'm Bob Henning. I'm calling to ask if anybody has reported anything strange in the area over the last hour or so."

The officer at the other end of the phone was nice, though somewhat amused by Bob's question.

"No, there've been no reports since I've been on duty. That's been a couple of hours. Why do you ask?"

"I saw something unusual," Bob replied, trying not to tip his hand, but coming across less a reporter and more a schizophrenic. About five seconds of silence passed.

"Okay. No, nothing going on here tonight." The officer never inquired about what Bob had seen and the wasted call ended.

The next day at his newspaper, the *Star Ledger* in Newark, Bob located the reporter who handled the Newark Airport area. He told the man the story and asked if he could put him in touch with somebody at the airport who might know something about strange flying phenomena and radar information. A phone call was arranged and questions were asked. Bob explained to the airport official that this was not a formal inquiry, but despite that, the airport official appeared willing to help. He said he would check into things and call Bob later the same day. He did.

"Essentially," the man noted, "we have no record of any aircraft flying in or around that location at that time that shouldn't have been there." Bob appreciated his help, but once off the phone, he wondered how such a large object avoided detection from modern radar.

Bob's next call was to McGuire Air Force Base, south of the sighting area. He believed their radar would confirm whether or not there was a strange flying object in the sky that night, or at least whether or not they had aircraft of their own flying in that neighborhood. But like most of the military's handling of the UFO question that phone call slammed into a fortified bunker.

"No, we have no information to give out, sir. But have you heard of this new group called MUFON?"

"I haven't," Bob said, "what's their story?"

The Air Force man told Bob about a blossoming investigative group known as MUFON (Mutual UFO Network). He recommended that Bob contact the organization and make an official report of his sighting. But after some consideration he decided against it.

The lack of radar reports from both the airport and the Air Force was consternation to a reporter's way of seeing reality. Assuming the object was solid and physical, it should have been tracked. It had been a large object in a busy sky. There was no way air traffic control should not have been aware of its presence. Air safety had been perforated and no one was talking about it.

From this point in the pre-digital world, Bob set out to learn as much about UFOs, their activities, histories, and missions as he could. But the more he studied, the less interested he became. Frankly, the entire topic turned him off. "I'm not getting involved with these people," was his fervent thought only a few cattle-mutilations and alien-abductions later.

Yet he knew what he saw. The triangular craft did not fit within the paradigm of normal social beliefs about credible aircraft. And if he had been alone in the car that night, he may never have talked about it. Huge, black, equilateral triangle-ship; without a corroborator, the incident would have been chalked off as hallucination. But he had help, important help, his wife's help. The incident was real, proved by the matching drawings he and Carol had laying on the kitchen table.

Despite the steadfastness of the craft in Bob's mind, he was not now a believer in UFOs. Skepticism was still a big part of his makeup, and he kept that practice close to the three-dimensional outline subscribed by mainstream science.

There was one problem, however.

In Bob's case, seeing the black ship became more than believing even though he did not know it, or would not, at the time, admit it. His mind had been permanently stretched by the three-pointed shape in a way that could not have been managed by any human-bound occurrence. And he could not retract the experience. So, no longer did his mind slam shut when stories from outside the box rolled his way. Rather, he gave them a wider birth and a closer inspection than he would have previously. Yet he maintained a leading edge of questions that demanded honest, common sense answers supported by physical reality. All this was fixed in the Life-of-Bob until twenty-seven years later in 2006.

Bob was watching the *Anderson Cooper 360°* show on CNN. The host was doing a comical report on the O'Hare Airport UFO sighting in Chicago of November 7, 2006. More startling to Bob than the report itself was the fact that CNN, whether serious or not, was giving expensive airtime to a UFO story.

With renewed interest Bob zipped to his laptop, surfed the internet for the O'Hare UFO incident, and began to study. He was impressed by the amount of data, the credibility of the witnesses, and the large number of airport personnel willing to confirm the sighting. Mostly, it was people from various airlines who refused to shut up about the incident because of their real concerns for their own and their co-workers safety in the air over O'Hare. In essence, after all his studies, he learned that it was not the type of case that anyone could dump as being unreasonable or unreal. Now, with renewed interest thanks to a news media battered by credible-witness-overload, and perhaps, his own added years of maturity and experience, Bob dove anew into the extraterrestrial question. He even joined a UFO group and has attended it three to four times a year since 2007.

For Bob, there is no one answer to the UFO phenomenon. There are probably a dozen answers that are all true. He doesn't believe that extraterrestrial intelligent life visits the earth. Rather, Bob is a fan of Jacques Vallee, international ufologist and author of numerous books, many of which espouse the idea that the aliens are here via different realities rather than different planets.

Did Bob see a UFO in 1979? He is still unsure, but is open to any correct answer. While being unidentified, the craft certainly was flying, but he is not convinced it was a solid physical object. He would concede that the object may have been a holographic projection as some other witnesses currently report (see: Holographic UFOs, davidicke.com). If not solid, this would explain two different radars' inability to pick it up on their screens (at least as far as airport and Air Force liaison people would recount to a newspaper inquiry). And it would explain why he could see stars through the ship's body.

Books, magazines, and videos, as well as firsthand accounts continue as part of his studies and hint at the massive number of possibilities outside our normal frontiers. They prop his mind ajar against the enormous weight of a conservative news-media. Bob is ready to turn the page for the follow-up stories.

CONCLUSION

This is my third book on UFOs. The conclusions are getting easier to write.
Aliens are here. They have apparently always been here.
Get used to it.

Human population is now (2013) over seven billion and rising, so it is increasingly difficult for the aliens to bounce around the planet without being noticed. We, too, travel more often and faster than in centuries past. And now, practically everyone carries a camera-phone in their pocket or purse. Also, the use of hypnotism breaks through alien-induced amnesia to varying degrees and spotlights their personal interference with citizens who, often, were not even aware of the intrusion (I am one of them). Their presence seems to be expanding exponentially as is the number of people admitting to having seen them.

The Age of Visitation is here.

Petition your congress-persons and senators to vote for an amendment to the United States Constitution that prohibits secrecy in the area of UFOs. All people on earth deserve to know the truth, and the United States breaking the silence would domino-effect other countries who have not already relaxed their denial programs, to quickly do so.

Are people ready for the truth?

Abraham Lincoln, 16th President of the United States, one of the more insightful and philosophical American leaders, thought so when he said, "I am a firm believer in the people. If given the truth, they can be depended upon to meet any national crisis. The great point is to bring them the *real facts*" [my italics].

This is certainly a truth. Look at New Jersey.

Faced with the irrefutable "truth" of Hurricane Sandy from October 22-31, 2012, they prepared, they got smashed, and they accepted the reality, but dove in to rebuild. By May of 2013, the Jersey shore was open for business again. (Remember their plucky motto? "New Jersey: Stronger than the Storm!")

They were presented the "real facts" and they met their regional crisis head-on. Across the country the "facts" of Sandy were embraced sparking nation-wide assistance to the Garden State.

Done.

How many examples are there where humans were slammed with real facts and handled them nobly? Japan after World War II? Hit with two Atom bombs, they recovered to become one of the leading economic powers on the planet. New York City after 9/11? Bounced right back, barely missing a step in the months that followed. How about you personally? After the death of a family member or friend, or a love relationship shattered by deceit, you met the crisis and continued.

Even if people are not ready for disclosure, they are. For even when folk perceive themselves as not ready, giving everyone the whole truth at one time would vindicate firsthand witnesses and staunch believers who had previously been thought of as "out there." That would generate a shift in human awareness that would push most moderately minded individuals towards acceptance of the facts, with the balance of the population eventually to follow. There would be almost no choice.

But convincing government leaders that disclosure is a good thing is like telling a five year old to give up that thirty-six ounce chocolate bar he's eating because it was meant to be shared. When you control the chocolate, sharing is a hard sell.

But if the government comes clean on the UFO question, will that return life to the Garden of Eden? No. Will some people remain obstinate, like the hard-core skeptics who say there is no conspiracy in the government to cover up UFOs? Sure, they will remain obstinate. Hard-core skeptics need their skepticism. It comforts them with a feeling of superiority. That allows them to feel safe, the most basic of human needs. And watch how fast that group joins the conspiracy side when officialdom is agin them. Even if the president himself introduced the skeptic crowd to a dozen aliens, they would claim it was all faked. Some folk like to argue.

As I end every UFO book, I urge the reader now to close the cover, hop in their car, and head-out to the suburban-rural lands tonight. Look for lights near the ground that seem misplaced. Stop your vehicle, get out, study the lights. Do they hover over a plowed field, or a lake, or thirty-feet up beside an evergreen; that is, are they in spots where it makes no sense to be? Do they constantly move in tight irregular patterns? And most important; are they there the next time you drive to that location? (If so, you missed; they are human-made. If not, hooray! It was a UFO!)

The proof is in the seeing.

See for yourself.

Gerard J. Medvec

APPENDIX

Kinds of Close Encounters

First kind
Seeing an unidentified flying object.

Second kind

Seeing an unidentified flying object, plus seeing physical evidence such as landing marks on the ground, chemical residue, or material debris.

Third kind

Seeing "occupants" in and/or around the UFO.

Fourth kind

A human is abducted by a UFO or its occupants.

Fifth kind

Contact with extraterrestrial intelligence that is human-initiated, conscious, and voluntary. It is a mutually agreed upon communication between human and alien.

General Reading Suggestions

Alien Agenda: Investigating the Extraterrestrial Presence Among Us
Jim Marrs (1997)

Breakthrough: The Next Step
Whitley Strieber (1995)

Chariots of the Gods
Erich Von Daniken (1999)

Communion: a True Story
Whitley Strieber (1987)

Dimensions: A Casebook of Alien Contact
Jacques Vallee (1988)

Fire in the Sky: The Walton Experience
Travis Walton (2010)

The Pine Bush Phenomenon
Vincent Polise (2005)

The Watchers
Raymond Fowler (1991)

Mid-Atlantic UFOs: High Traffic Area
Gerard Medvec (2013)

UFOs Above Pennsylvania
Mark Sarro and Gerard Medvec (2013)

RESOURCES

apod.nasa.gov/apod/ap060117.html – roll clouds

http://answers.yahoo.com/question/index?qid=20100127164916AAxXDyq – radar altitude

http://corbin-law-office.com/services/aviation-law/ – FAA Administration action

http://hq-web03.ita.doc.gov/License/Surge.nsf/webfiles/SteelMillDevelopments/ – steel industry figures

http://www.aopa.org/News-and-Video/All-News/2013/May/29/Preserving-a-lost-art-Formation-flying-goes-mainstream.aspx – FAA regulation 14 CFR 91.111 Operating near other aircraft

http://news.stanford.edu/news/2009/june3/birds-060309.html – airplane flight formation

International UFO Museum and Research Center, Roswell, New Mexico – all short reports

library.thinkquest.org/C0122781/psychology/stages.htm – Emotional Stages of a Dying Person

mufon.com/ – Mutual UFO Network – monthly UFO sightings reports

Strieber, Whitley. *Communion: A True Story.* New York, NY: Avon Books, 1988

The National UFO Reporting Center (www.ufocenter.com) – all short reports

www.airliners.net/aviation-forums/tech_ops

www.brainyquote.com/quotes/authors – all quotes

www.en.wikipedia.org – various

www.flyngo.com/pilots-handbook-aeronautical-knowledge

www.hypertextbook.com – g-force info

www.jaunted.com/story/ – Pine Bush, NY UFO history

www.medscape.com/features/slideshow/hysteria

www.phschool.com/science/science_news – "Anatomy of a Lightning Ball"

www.presentationmall.com – map of New Jersey

www.psychologytoday.com/blog/intense-emotions-and-strong-feelings/

www.science.howstuffworks.com – g-force info

www.ufocasebook.com/Pineywoods – The Cash-Landrum Incident

www.ufofiler.com   Filer's Files – all short reports

www.unep.org/Documents.Multilingual/Default.asp?DocumentID=2649&Article – United Nations Environmental Protection info

www.wired.com/wiredscience/2009/08/morninggloryclouds/

Gerard J. Medvec has authored *Mid-Atlantic UFOS*, co-authored *Ghosts of Delaware* and *UFOs Above PA* with Mark Sarro (Schiffer Publishing), and published over sixty non-fiction articles and five short stories. He studied communications at Delaware County Community College in Pennsylvania, and with the Newspaper Institute of American in New York. His interests in the paranormal began at age five with an alien phenomenon. He participated in the Gateway Voyager program, an experiential study in altered-states, at the Monroe Institute in Faber, Virginia. UFOs have been "regulars" in his life for over fifty-five years. He resides with his wife, Joyce, in Delaware City, Delaware.